lovers

LINDA SUNSHINE

Turner Publishing, Inc.

**This book is dedicated, with love, to my dear cousin,
Ronnie Hoffman, for her generous spirit, her wicked sense of humor, and for all the hours
we spent together at the movies.**

The author wishes to thank the many people who helped transform this project from a romantic idea to a real book:

First, to my best friend, most consistent supporter, and extraordinary agent, Lena Tabori; to Michael Reagan at Turner Publishing for giving me the opportunity (and the excuse) to watch movies all day; to Nai Chang for his brilliant sense of style, his patience for endless editorial changes, and many late night dinners; to Jennifer Downing for laughing in all the right places and for her persistence in losing every annoying widow; to Richard Ackerman and Daniel Eagan for sharing their vast knowledge of movies and for their dedication to accuracy; to Larry Larson, who brings good cheer to the tedious details; to Ross Horowitz for helping with the research; and to everyone at Turner Publishing and Andrews and McMeel, including the sales reps, who gave this book the best possible send-off.

And, finally, to the Leadman, for writing the book on proximal tension, among other things.

LINDA SUNSHINE

Turner Publishing would like to thank the following people for helping to make the book possible: Ted Turner, Scott Sassa, Ira Miskin, Roger Mayer, Dick May, Woolsey Ackerman, Larry Larson, Cathy Manolis, Susan Tungate, Barbara Swint, and Jennifer Falk-Weiss.

MICHAEL REAGAN

Published by Turner Publishing, Inc.
A Division of Turner Broadcasting System, Inc.
One CNN Center, Atlanta, Georgia 30348

© 1992 by Turner Publishing, Inc.

Produced by Welcome Enterprises, Inc.
164 East 95th Street, New York, New York 10128

Project Director: Lena Tabori
Project Manager: Hiro Clark
Managing Editor: Jennifer Downing
Designer: Nai Chang
Editor: Robin Jacobson

Distributed by Andrews and McMeel
A Universal Press Syndicate Company
4900 Main Street, Kansas City, Missouri 64112

Permissions and copyright notices appear on page 200.

ISBN: 1-878685-03-1

Library of Congress Catalog Card Number: 91-75252

First edition
10 9 8 7 6 5 4 3 2 1

Printed and bound in Japan by Toppan Printing, Co., Inc.

PREFACE

This book examines the great love teams in American movies, and explores the ways in which movies affect our concept of love and romance. Many of our romantic illusions come from the movies, so it is interesting to address some of the fundamental questions about screen lovers: Where does fantasy end and reality begin for these actors? What's the difference between an on-screen love affair and an offscreen relationship? Can married actors work together?

Lovers includes sixteen of Hollywood's best-known couples. Obviously, they were chosen from many possible candidates. As in any book of this type, the choices were partly arbitrary, but each couple chosen best symbolizes one aspect of romance as it has traditionally been portrayed by Hollywood.

All the couples were selected also because they had accumulated a major body of work. It may seem odd to omit from a book about screen lovers such famous couples as Clark Gable and Vivien Leigh (*Gone with the Wind*) or Humphrey Bogart and Ingrid Bergman (*Casablanca*). However, couples who only made one movie together were not included, as their collaboration could be argued to have been something of a one-night stand. Would Gable and Leigh have made magic in a contemporary drama? We'll never know.

The couples in this book, on the other hand, have withstood the test of time. Of course, in each case their cumulative work had its peaks and valleys, its triumphs and disappointments, just as in any long-term relationship. Yet, for the most part, their movies are still popular today, and some of these couples are still producing high-quality work.

Individual preferences vary, of course, but these couples encompass almost every movie fantasy. They are the screen lovers who have brought our dreams to life. What's your dream? Twirling around a dance floor with Fred Astaire? Sharing a cigarette with Garbo? Sailing the high seas with Clark Gable? Singing with Judy Garland? Being tested with brain twisters by Spencer Tracy? Gulping martinis with William Powell? Lingering under a magnolia tree with Joanne Woodward? Trading anxiety attacks with Woody Allen? According to Hollywood, all these fantasies are possible for the token price of a movie ticket. It's no wonder, then, that we're addicted to the movies.

LINDA SUNSHINE
February 1991

CONTENTS

INTRODUCTION

Movies have always reflected the morals, the hopes, and the dreams of the public. Into this larger-than-life medium we cast our wildest fantasies and our deepest desires. In the darkness of the theater we rediscover ourselves. Life, as projected through a movie camera, fulfills our longings. In *Annie Hall* Woody Allen says: "You're always trying to get things to come out perfectly in art because it's real difficult in life."

Romance has always played a major role in the movies. Our ideas about love and relationships have been shaped by the lovers we see on the screen. We admire and try to emulate them. Almost every movie genre—love stories, mysteries, thrillers, westerns, swashbucklers, war and gangster tales—has a structure that features a leading man and a leading woman, so thousands of different couples exist on film. But relatively few couples have had real magic. Fred Astaire, for example, made many films with various leading ladies, but most of his enduring classics costarred Ginger Rogers.

Determining what makes a perfect screen couple is as difficult as understanding what makes a successful relationship in real life. Sometimes two people are the same type, such as perennial teenagers Mickey Rooney and Judy Garland. Conversely, opposites attract, such as when nebbish Woody Allen and the gorgeous Diane Keaton fall for each other. Great screen couples, like all great lovers, share an element of mystery and wonder. "We're inevitable," John Gilbert tells Greta Garbo in *Queen Christina*, "Don't you feel it?" She does, and so do we. Great lovers always seem inevitable, part kismet and part coinci-

dence. We may not understand how or why they seem so perfect, but we know them when we see them. And how we love to see them.

Today, an estimated twenty-two million people go to the movies once a week, but in 1946, when the population was considerably smaller, an astonishing ninety million people went at least that often. To the public, actors became the characters they portrayed on screen. Women identified with Joan Crawford, for example, because she always played the working girl who made good. And in real life (as glamorized by the MGM publicity department), Crawford had risen from poverty and a broken home to reign, beautiful and successful beyond imagination, as queen of Hollywood. "It's not who you are, it's what you are that counts," as she says in *Dance, Fools, Dance.* Indeed, you can change what you are, if not who. Crawford's image made it seem as if the dream might come down off the screen and transform the lives of her fans.

Certainly, Crawford had "star quality," an attribute essential for both partners of a successful screen couple and, at the same time, so difficult to define. In a recent television interview, Katharine Hepburn was asked what it takes to be a star. "I don't think it's talent," she replied. "You've got to have a good hot motor inside you, and it ticks away, and your eyes shine and your teeth shine."

Perhaps it's that good hot motor ticking away inside that draws an audience to an actor. Certainly, it's not just looks. Tracy was decidedly chunky, Astaire was all angles, and Bogart could be considered borderline ugly. Yet, though far from tall, dark, and handsome, they are among the most popular and enduring actors of all time. Legions of fans still rent videotapes of their movies and watch them on television.

And fans identified not only with particular actors, but with particular screen couples. In the '30s and '40s, movies were controlled by the heads of the major studios. Contract actors were virtually enslaved to executives such as Louis B. Mayer at MGM and Jack Warner at Warner Brothers. If an actor and an actress were successful together in a film, it was likely they would be recast as a team, especially if they were both under contract to the same studio. If they proved popular in two films, the studio would have scripts written to fit their personalities, and there was no limit on the number of times they would be rematched. Thus, Myrna Loy and William Powell, the quintessential happily married couple of the '40s, made fourteen films together in as many years.

Each successful Hollywood screen couple was popular in its own way. Putting two people together created a third entity, a single ideal. Greta Garbo and John Gilbert embodied temptation in its most passionate, and often self-destructive, form. Jean Harlow and Clark Gable sparked lust; Fred Astaire and Ginger Rogers personified elegance and class; Judy Garland and Mickey Rooney spelled good, clean fun; Clark Gable and Joan Crawford radiated glamour; and Spencer Tracy and Katharine Hepburn always projected genuine affection and admiration. Moviegoers longed for these kinds of relationships, these ideals that seemed so attainable on screen and so impossible in real life.

What made these couples so appealing? Certainly, it had to do, at least partly, with the times. Greer Garson and Walter Pidgeon, loving each other and enduring the hardships of World War II in *Mrs. Miniver* were a couple who people wanted and needed to see on the screen. But the common bond and the lasting appeal of the majority of screen couples from this era also had to do with equality of the sexes.

We may think of the liberated woman as a phenomenon of the '70s, but just look at the female characters of the '30s and '40s. Here were women who stood up to their men. Women who could wisecrack, work, even fight, if necessary, for the things they wanted and for the men they loved. Equal partners in solving a crime, running a business, singing operetta, or dancing on Broadway, they put up with rivals and took it on the chin; they were sometimes down but never out. "I've made a mistake," Crawford tells Gable in *Laughing Sinners*. "I've stumbled and fallen, but I'm not throwing myself away." Of course she's not. "From now on I'm going to be the one doing the chasing," Loy warns Powell in *I Love You Again*, "and, believe me, you'll know you've been chased." We believe her.

These women kept up with their men in the bedroom, the boardroom, and even the barroom, when need be. In *China Seas* a jealous, seething Harlow says to the waiter: "Get on the belt line and keep 'em coming." In *Woman of the Year* Tracy says: "Make mine a double," and Hepburn doesn't hesitate for a moment. "Me, too," she says. "Don't worry about me. As a diplomat's daughter, I've had to match drinks with a lot of people, from remittance men to international spies, and, I may say, I've never wound up under the table." And perhaps the best example is in *The Thin Man*:

NORA: Say, how many drinks have you had?
NICK: This will make six martinis.
NORA (*to waiter*): All right. Will you bring me five more
          martinis, Leo, and line them right up here.

These women matched their men, drink for drink, and in every other way, and the men loved them for it. They were true equals, which is perhaps the reason screen idols such as Marilyn Monroe, Marlon Brando, James Dean, and Bette Davis were never part of a couple. When one person is too powerful, his or her presence overwhelms any potential mate. Bette Davis acted all her leading men right off the screen. And who could take their eyes off Marilyn Monroe long enough to even notice her partner?

Tracy and Hepburn, who were perhaps the epitome of equality among the sexes, did not have this problem. In many of their movies, he's a confirmed bachelor until she amazes him with her smarts and dazzles him with her wit, winning his heart in the last reel. In *Woman of the Year*, Tracy declares his love, and Hepburn asks: "Even

10

when I'm sober?" He replies: "Even when you're brilliant." Though these screen relationships were extremely powerful, things began to change by the late '40s, when most of the popular pairings, with the exception of Tracy and Hepburn, had dissolved. Despite some encore performances, it became more likely that a leading actor or actress would have a different co-star for every new film. This was partly due to changes made in the studio system after the war. Television shows became a financially more viable format for couples such as Lucille Ball and Desi Arnaz, and George Burns and Gracie Allen.

Perhaps this explains why moviegoers became even more fascinated with actors and actresses who were married in real life. The Bogarts, the Oliviers, the Burtons, and the Newmans captured the attention of the public, and stories about them swept through the newspapers. Here were couples whose real lives were as glamorous as their celluloid fantasies. The Bogarts, the seminal couple of the late '40s, were photographed in nightclubs and seen on television in an idyllic home setting with their two children. The Oliviers—gorgeous, talented, and titled—were admired on two continents and were as close to royalty as any fan could wish. The Burtons thrilled fans with their stormy relationship and were hounded by the international press, who furtively photographed them on their yacht and in various exotic retreats. Only the Newmans managed a semblance of normal life, keeping out of the public eye except to make public statements on political issues.

These couples generated publicity wherever they went, and their fame made it possible for them to work together. However, when married couples work together, usually either their work or their relationship suffers. Ironically, married actors almost never make their best movies with their mates. Perhaps this is the fault of celebrity taking precedence over quality of work. In October 1968, in an article for *Esquire*, Wilfrid Sheed discussed "whether husbands and wives should ever work together," reaching the conclusion that, for Taylor and Burton, "surely couples shouldn't act together where the differential in talent is as great as this . . . they simply fall down on top of each other."

But the publicity given to the private lives of these couples generated enough interest to guarantee the success of their movies, regardless of the quality of their work. Fans flocked to their films to see what they would look like on the screen. Bogart and Bacall made four movies together, and all were inferior to his work with actresses such as Ingrid Bergman and Katharine Hepburn. In fact, the only interesting parts of Bogart's movies with Bacall were their scenes together. The Oliviers only made three movies together, and one of them, *21 Days Together,* was so bad it wasn't even released until they were both major stars. Yet Vivien Leigh and Laurence Olivier separately made some of the greatest movies ever produced in Hollywood. Joanne Woodward and Paul Newman costarred in ten films and except for *The Long, Hot Summer* and *Mr. & Mrs. Bridge* their movies are eminently forgettable.

The Burtons were perhaps the most extreme example. They costarred in several bombs (with the possible exception of *Who's Afraid of Virginia Woolf?*), yet for years their movies made money based solely on their star status. For a while it seemed as though the public would watch anything with Liz and Dick, but, after being assaulted with films such as *Boom!* and *Under Milk Wood,* even their staunchest fans rebelled. The Burtons' working relationship came to an end, and so did their marriage.

Perhaps married people shouldn't work together, but longtime lovers may be another story. Though Katharine Hepburn and Spencer Tracy were part of the studio system of the '30s and '40s, they were unique in several important ways. They maintained a personal relationship that, for the most part, was kept out of the press, and were the only couple of their generation to survive the studio system, continuing to collaborate right up until Tracy's death in the late '60s. Partners on screen and off, they made both relationships work.

The same can be said for Woody Allen who, in the past twenty years, has maintained two long-term personal relationships with leading ladies Diane Keaton and Mia Farrow. Of course, Allen is more than just an actor. In his way, he is one of the few filmmakers who make movies in the repertory tradition of the studio system, using the same people over and over again. And his work is so personal we often think we know more about his private life than we actually do.

It is hard to separate real life from fantasy when the couple on the screen is also a couple in real life. We can't help but wonder how much of the actors' private lives are being projected onto their screen characters. Actually, most of the time we don't want to know. We go to the movies to escape, to lose ourselves, to be someone else.

In the early days of Hollywood, moviemakers set out to create pure fantasies. Thus, the films of Fred Astaire and Ginger Rogers glorified a carefree life of wealth and privilege during the most severe depression this country has ever known. Yet people believed such a life existed, and they longed to be part of it.

Inevitably, we compare our lives to those of the actors and actresses we see on the screen. We can't help measuring the real world against the fantasy, and our lives always seem a little smaller for it. "It's only a movie," we say, but deep down we don't believe it. Somewhere in the back of our minds we believe that in real life Loy and Powell or Garson and Pidgeon would stay happily married forever. And wanting to believe is almost the same as believing.

These couples reinforce our fantasies, and we love them for it. How we root for our heroes and heroines! Just when Harlow thinks she's lost Gable forever in *Hold Your Man*, he turns and says: "Wait a minute, darling, you ain't gonna cry on your wedding day?"

"Ah! Sweet mystery of life," as Jeanette MacDonald and Nelson Eddy crooned. And the mystery is this: Why can't real life work like the movies?

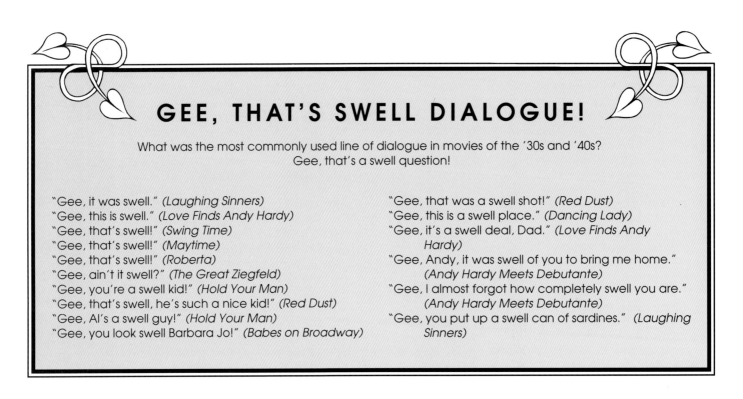

GEE, THAT'S SWELL DIALOGUE!

What was the most commonly used line of dialogue in movies of the '30s and '40s?
Gee, that's a swell question!

"Gee, it was swell." *(Laughing Sinners)*
"Gee, this is swell." *(Love Finds Andy Hardy)*
"Gee, that's swell!" *(Swing Time)*
"Gee, that's swell!" *(Maytime)*
"Gee, that's swell!" *(Roberta)*
"Gee, ain't it swell?" *(The Great Ziegfeld)*
"Gee, you're a swell kid!" *(Hold Your Man)*
"Gee, that's swell, he's such a nice kid!" *(Red Dust)*
"Gee, Al's a swell guy!" *(Hold Your Man)*
"Gee, you look swell Barbara Jo!" *(Babes on Broadway)*

"Gee, that was a swell shot!" *(Red Dust)*
"Gee, this is a swell place." *(Dancing Lady)*
"Gee, it's a swell deal, Dad." *(Love Finds Andy Hardy)*
"Gee, Andy, it was swell of you to bring me home." *(Andy Hardy Meets Debutante)*
"Gee, I almost forgot how completely swell you are." *(Andy Hardy Meets Debutante)*
"Gee, you put up a swell can of sardines." *(Laughing Sinners)*

PART ONE

lovers on screen

temptation
GARBO & GILBERT

"My boy, when the devil cannot reach us through the spirit . . .
he creates a woman beautiful enough to reach us through the flesh."

FLESH AND THE DEVIL (1926)

There never was—and probably never will be—a screen presence equal to that of Greta Garbo. She was the standard against which all other actresses were measured, and perhaps still are. John Barrymore, her costar in *Grand Hotel,* once said: "Garbo has only to flash on screen to seize our attention. Her brilliance dispels our dullness. It isn't acting. It is something that holds us in its spell. A kind of magic."

Certainly, Garbo's magic was unique. Clarence Brown, who directed her in several films, said: "There was something behind the eye that told the whole story. She could be looking in this direction, in a close-up at somebody whom she despised, and you could see it in her eyes. And she could turn across to the camera, to her love, without a change of expression, but it was there. Nobody ever had that . . . on the screen but Garbo."

Among a handful of screen idols who have fascinated generations of movie fans, "she played heroines that were at once sensual and pure, superficial and profound, suffering and hopeful, world-weary and life inspiring," writes movie critic Ephraim Katz. "On the screen as off, she represented a remote figure of loveliness—aloof, enigmatic, craving to be alone." In her sixteen-year career, Garbo made only twenty-four films, yet when she retired, she was a screen legend.

Born Greta Louisa Gustafsson in 1905, in Stockholm, she was the daughter of a laborer, who died when Greta was an adolescent. "I can't remember being young, really young, like other children," she once said.

Flesh and the Devil featured John Gilbert, "The Great Lover" of silent films, and Greta Garbo, "The Swedish Sphinx."

She had a brief career as a model before catching the eye of famed European director Mauritz Stiller. He wanted to mold her into the perfect woman. Stiller showed her how to dress, how to wear makeup, and how to act. And he christened her "Greta Garbo."

When Louis B. Mayer offered Stiller an MGM contract in 1924, the director insisted that Mayer also sign up his protégé. Mayer reluctantly agreed, saying: "Tell her in America men don't like fat women."

Garbo arrived in Hollywood the next year, at the age of nineteen. She didn't speak English, and she looked like a laundress when compared to such stars as Gloria Swanson, Clara Bow, and Lillian Gish. Garbo dropped twenty pounds, and MGM remade her image, tweezing her eyebrows, straightening her hair, and capping her teeth. They assigned their best cinematographer, William H. Daniels, to her. (He later said she had no bad angles.) Then, MGM featured Garbo in two silent films, *The Torrent* and *The Temptress.* Audiences were captivated by her exotic, ravishing beauty. "This girl has everything," claimed *Variety.* The only thing she lacked was a strong leading man.

"The Swedish Sphinx" met her match in John Gilbert, who was known as "The Great Lover." Born in 1897, Gilbert had begun his film career in 1916, appearing in westerns until he moved up to the role of "the other man" in melodramas. In 1924, when his contract with Fox expired, he was signed by MGM. The studio wanted to capitalize on his dark, Valentino-like looks and his expressive eyes, which could convey both passion and compassion. In 1925, he starred in *The Big Parade,* which ran for two years in New York's Astor Theater and grossed more than $15 million.

MGM's famed cinematographer, William Daniels, said that Garbo was most alluring
when reclining, and he often shot her in that position. In this boudoir scene from *Flesh and the Devil*
Garbo and Gilbert created a new standard for screen passion.

Gilbert was twenty-nine years old and at his peak as a silent-screen star when MGM paired him with Greta Garbo, then twenty-one, in *Flesh and the Devil*, which was destined to become a landmark film. They met on the set right before filming a scene in which they were to make love in Garbo's boudoir. As she lounged on a divan with his head resting on her stomach, the physical attraction between them was so obvious that director Clarence Brown later admitted he was embarrassed to call "cut." Instead, he and his six-man crew quietly turned off the cameras and lights and retreated from the sound stage, leaving Garbo and Gilbert to carry on the scene in private. Brown then went to Mayer and said: "I think we've got the greatest romantic couple that has ever appeared in films. . . . This is more than celluloid romance; this is the real thing."

In *Flesh and the Devil*, Garbo devoured Gilbert with kisses. Their garden tryst became an erotic dalliance, as she suggestively twirled a cigarette between her lips. In a church scene, she transformed a sip from a Communion cup into a profane innuendo. It's no wonder, then, that in the film Garbo's beauty overwhelmed Gilbert, and that he sinned. *Photoplay* called their love scenes "smolderingly fervent," and the critic for the *New York Herald-Tribune* wrote: "Frankly,

"My only excuse is I love you," Garbo tells Gilbert in *Flesh and the Devil*, explaining why she, a married woman, has seduced him into an illicit affair. On screen and off, Garbo was ever the temptress, a role to which she proved perfectly suited.

"Forget you? Not while I live, not if I die!" Gilbert vows in *Flesh and the Devil*. Offscreen, he was just as ardent in pursuing Garbo and was crushed when she repeatedly rejected his marriage proposals.

never in our screen career have we seen seduction so perfectly done. . . . Greta Garbo . . . is the personification of passion."

Offscreen as well, the couple fell in love, and Garbo moved into Gilbert's Hollywood mansion. It was clear to everyone on the set that he was madly infatuated with her. He could scarcely wait to finish a scene before rushing off to her dressing room. He called her "Flicka" and extolled her as "the most alluring creature you have ever seen. Capricious as the devil, whimsical, temperamental and fascinating. . . . What a woman! One day she is childlike, naive, ingenious, a girl of ten. The next day she is a mysterious woman a thousand years old, knowing everything, baffled deep. Garbo has more sides to her than anyone I have ever met!"

Gilbert was desperate to marry Garbo, but she left him standing at the altar three times. He told a reporter:

"She keeps saying 'you're in love with Garbo the actress' and, you know, I say 'you're damned right.'"

She was more reticent than he in talking to the press. Her last extensive interview was in 1928, when she told reporter Ruth Biery: "Your joys and sorrows, you never can tell them. You cheapen yourself on the inside when you tell them." She refused to discuss her relationship with Gilbert, just as she would refuse to discuss her personal life for the next sixty years.

Their affair sent Gilbert into a mental decline. He took to drinking heavily and to offending the MGM brass. He was one of the studio's hottest properties, "but he was the one member of the MGM family whom Mayer hated the most," writes author Jane Wayne. "One reason was (his relationship with) Garbo, who not only followed Gilbert's advice in money matters but threatened to become an American citizen by marrying John when Mayer wanted to have her deported for

cede to her demands because they wanted her for *Love,* a modernized and decidedly loose adaptation of Tolstoy's novel *Anna Karenina.* Gilbert was cast as Vronsky, and publicity for the film proclaimed: "John Gilbert and Greta Garbo in *Love.*" (The picture was originally titled *Heat,* which also would have made for an interesting tag line.)

The success of *Love* led to *A Woman of Affairs,* another silent film, in 1928. As the opening dialogue card reads, it was "the story of a gallant lady—a lady who was perhaps foolish and reckless beyond need—but withal a very gallant lady." In her first contemporary role, Garbo was cast as a doomed flapper. "Once a

Left and above:
Garbo and Gilbert in *Love.* He's a dashing officer, and she's the alluring wife of a tyrant in this silent-screen adaptation of *Anna Karenina.* The emotional subtlety of her acting was far ahead of its time, especially for audiences accustomed to the exaggerated facial expressions of most silent-screen actors. The critic Kenneth Tynan once wrote: "What when drunk one sees in other women, one sees in Garbo when sober."

In *A Woman of Affairs* Garbo comes out of her mad delirium when Gilbert visits her in the sanatorium. The happy expression on her face quickly changes once she turns to see Gilbert's wife standing in the corner.

failing to show up at the studio. Many guests at the wedding of Eleanor Boardman and King Vidor in 1926 heard Mayer say to Gilbert when Garbo's name was mentioned, 'What do you have to marry her for? Why don't you just fuck her and forget about it?' Gilbert pounced on his boss with both fists, and the two men drew blood. The other guests pulled them apart. When Mayer got to his feet holding a pair of broken eyeglasses, he shouted, 'You're through Gilbert! I'll destroy you if it costs me a million dollars!'" It was a promise that Mayer eventually kept.

At the time, Gilbert was earning $10,000 a week, as compared to Garbo's $600. She demanded $5,000, and when Mayer refused she sailed to Sweden, where she remained for seven months. MGM was forced to

man loves her—he never forgets her," reads another card. Though Gilbert is married, Garbo tempts him into reviving their love affair. She's redeemed in the end, when she gives him up and then dies in a car accident.

The film represented a turning point for both actors. She ended their affair after this production, for reasons she never discussed.

While shooting her next film, *Wild Orchids*, Garbo learned that Stiller, at the age of forty-five, had died of a heart attack; he was found still clutching a photograph of her. And during this time the careers of all silent film stars were suddenly jeopardized by the advent of talking movies. Thus, both Garbo and Gilbert had cause to be anxious.

Everyone at MGM was nervous about Garbo's future in the talkies. She was kept in silent films until 1930, two years longer than any other MGM star of her stature. The studio gave her extra time to learn English and perfect her accent. They needn't have worried; Garbo's voice was meant for talking pictures. She caused a sensation with her speaking debut in *Anna Christie* when she uttered her famous first line: "Give me a visky with ginger ale on the side—and don't be stingy, baby!" Her deep, melancholy voice was distinctively exotic and titillatingly masculine. Audiences responded enthusiastically. The MGM slogan "Garbo talks!" lives on even today.

Gilbert didn't fare nearly as well. In *The Hollywood Revue of 1929* he performed the balcony scene from

Opposite and above:
In *A Woman of Affairs* Garbo and Gilbert take a ride in the country and share a kiss under their special tree.
In real life, the film marked the end of their relationship. For reasons she never
revealed, Garbo stopped seeing Gilbert after this film was shot.

When Garbo and Gilbert meet in *Queen Christina*, he doesn't know she's a queen. He also doesn't know she's a woman, a fact that is soon revealed when they are forced to share a bed.

Romeo and Juliet with Norma Shearer, and audiences snickered at his high-pitched voice. It was rumored that MGM, on orders from Mayer himself, had tampered with the microphones. But Gilbert's voice was not his only problem. As Ephraim Katz has pointed out: "Possibly the most important factor contributing to his downfall was that the type of passionate romantic drama that made him so popular went out of style at the close of the silent era, and he wasn't a good enough actor to make an easy adjustment to a new type of role." In any case, Gilbert's career plummeted, as did his personal life. His two-year marriage to Ina Claire ended in divorce, and he began drinking with abandon. He starred in a few other vehicles that didn't do well. Then, he took out an ad in the trades that read: "MGM will neither offer me work nor release me from my contract. Signed John Gilbert." The impetuous act only hurt his diminishing reputation in Hollywood.

Although Garbo's film career continued to soar, her reputation as the woman who wanted to be alone plagued her. She was decidedly unhappy living in California. In sixteen years she moved eleven times, unable to find a place to call her own. She refused to play the Hollywood game—she didn't go to premieres or give autographs. She continually threatened to leave movies altogether.

While working, though, she was the quintessential professional: always on time, always prepared, but not without certain idiosyncrasies. She insisted on a closed set and demanded that black screens be placed around the sound stage so she wouldn't see the director, the cameras, or any of the crew. She wore carpet slippers in any scene during which the camera did not show her feet. Before going on the set, she would always ask her director: "Is the feet in?"

She was granted leeway because, with each screen appearance, the legend of her grew. By 1932, she was at the height of her commercial success, having made headlines with such films as *Mata Hari* and *Grand Hotel*. Her contract with MGM expired, and she spoke of retiring. MGM offered her $7,000 a week, but she held out for $10,000, once again retreating to Sweden until her demands were met. She returned for a two-picture deal, the studio allowing her to choose one of them. Her choice was *Queen Christina*, the story of the seventeenth-century Swedish queen who abdicates her throne for love. Having script and cast approval, Garbo rejected Laurence Olivier as her costar and insisted that MGM cast John Gilbert in the role of Antonio, the Spanish envoy who steals the queen's heart. "'Now I Help You,' Says Garbo to Gilbert," proclaimed a headline in *Photoplay*. "Who will say that royalty knows no gratitude—or that Garbo lacks warm human feeling?" concluded the article, speculating that Garbo was repaying Gilbert for favors granted her in the past. In any event, *Queen Christina* was their final film together.

To the role of Christina, Garbo brought her signature brand of androgyny. As the Swedish chancellor (played by Lewis Stone) reports, the King has "brought up this child as a boy, accustomed her ears to the sound of cannon fire, and sought to mold her spirit after his own." Garbo rides her horse as fiercely as any man, and she refuses to accept any of her numerous marriage proposals. "But your majesty cannot die an old maid," warns the chancellor. "I have no intention to," counters Garbo. "I shall die a bachelor."

She wears pants, wide-brimmed hats, and high collars. Her hair is cut in a severe pageboy. It's no wonder, then, that Gilbert mistakes her for a young man

when they meet in the woods. In the next scene, they meet at an inn, and are asked to share the only available room. She hesitates at first, but then agrees. When she reveals herself to be a woman, Gilbert does one of his silent screen double takes and then says: "Of course. It had to be. I felt it. A presence. Oh, life can be so gloriously improbable."

They spend three days together, and Garbo is finally in love—as a woman, not as a queen. But her subjects rebel at the thought of a Spaniard for a king.

The Spanish envoy, Gilbert, discovers that Garbo is Queen Christina when he arrives at court. Lewis Stone (who would later play Dad to Mickey Rooney's Andy Hardy) hands Gilbert a document. *Queen Christina* was the final film that Garbo and Gilbert made together. The movie did little to boost his faltering career, but it greatly enhanced the Garbo mystique.

"Evidently my people, who are said to love me, do not want me to be happy," concludes the queen. So she gives up her throne. The abdication scene proved prophetic, as Garbo herself retired from Hollywood a

23

Garbo's elusive screen persona remained a mystery to her fans as well as the people who knew her personally. Eleanor Boardman, wife of MGM director King Vidor, noted: "You can't pigeon-hole Garbo, she was fascinating. Extremely selfish, beautiful, strange . . . she was like Chaplin; she was man, woman and child."

few years later. "All my life I have been a symbol," says Queen Christina. "A symbol is eternal, changeless, an abstraction. A human being is mortal and changeable with desires and impulses, hopes and despair. I'm tired of being a symbol. I long to be a human being. This longing I cannot suppress. . . . One must live for oneself. After all, one's life is all one has. . . ."

It could be said that Garbo left Hollywood for the same reasons, abdicating her role as the screen's most alluring goddess. "There is a voice in our souls which tells us what to do, and we obey. I have no choice," says Queen Christina.

Garbo retired in 1941, at the age of thirty-six, thereby cementing her image as the ultimate unattain-

able woman. "Why did you give up the movies?" David Niven once asked her. "I had made enough faces," she replied.

Garbo never married. She lived out her life in seclusion, shrouded in mystery and timeless in her beauty. Perhaps she was always misunderstood.

"I never said I want to be left alone, I only said I want to be *let* alone. There is all the difference," Garbo once told a friend. Garbo died in April 1990, at the age of eighty-five. She was still as much a mystery as ever.

She had, at least, ended her career by her own choosing. Gilbert ended his under much more tragic circumstances. Though *Queen Christina* was well received, most of the praise went to Garbo and director Rouben Mamoulian. Gilbert's performance did little to bolster his sinking career.

After *Queen Christina*, MGM cast John Gilbert opposite rising star Jean Harlow in *Red Dust*. According to John Lee Mahin, who wrote the script: "Harlow was supposed to help Gilbert's fading image. Gilbert had a high, squeaky voice, and was too thin from drinking and everything else, and nervous because he was unsure of himself. If she liked him, maybe it would help. . . . Then I saw a screening of a new Gable film. . . . I went to Hunt (Stromberg, the film's supervisor) and said, 'There's this guy, my God, he's got the eyes of a woman and the build of a bull. He's really going to be something. . . . He and Harlow will be a natural,' and Hunt said: 'By God, you're right.'"

Thus, Gilbert lost his last chance to regain his star status in Hollywood. Then, his fourth marriage ended in divorce, and Columbia gave him fourth billing in *The Captain Hates the Sea* in 1934. Gilbert gave an ironically convincing performance as a drunken Hollywood writer, as he was intoxicated during most of the shoot. By 1936, at the age of thirty-nine, he had drunk himself to death.

"The Great Lover" had fallen from grace. "The Swedish Sphinx" had stepped off her pedestal. It could be said that, as a screen couple, Garbo and Gilbert symbolized opposite ends of Hollywood's precarious seesaw of fame.

TYPICAL LOVE SCENE
Greta Garbo and John Gilbert

Most love scenes between Garbo and Gilbert take place in complete silence. Yet even without dialogue, their passion smolders from the screen. *Queen Christina* is the only talkie they made. The following scene takes place in a country inn, where Garbo and Gilbert have spent three snowbound days. He doesn't yet know that she is queen of Sweden and that their time together has been especially precious to her. She has just spent several minutes examining every object in the room.

GILBERT: What are you doing?

GARBO: I've been memorizing the room. In the future, in my memory, I shall live a great deal in this room.

GILBERT: You wait, I'll show you the whole living world.

GARBO: I have imagined happiness but happiness you cannot imagine. Happiness you must feel, joy you must feel. Oh, and this great joy I feel now. . . . This is how the Lord must have felt when he first walked the finished world with all his creatures breathing, living. (*They kiss.*)

GILBERT: And to think a few snowdrifts might have separated us forever.

GARBO: We might have been born in different centuries.

GILBERT: No, I never would have permitted that. We're inevitable, don't you feel it?

GARBO: I feel it. But how can you be so sure? You know me so little.

GILBERT: That's true. There's a mystery in you.

GARBO: Is there not in every human being?

GILBERT: . . . Ah, to have found anyone in this wilderness would have been miracle enough but to have found you—this is too improbable. I don't believe in you. You're an illusion. You'll vanish before my eyes.

FILMOGRAPHY

Flesh and the Devil (1926)   *A Woman of Affairs* (1928)
Love (1927)   *Queen Christina* (1933)

Lust
GABLE & HARLOW

"I've been looking at her kind ever since my voice changed."

Clark Gable, about Jean Harlow,
RED DUST (1932)

Jean Harlow and Clark Gable were two of a kind—earthy and sexual, with a penchant for the cutting wisecrack. She was the sultry platinum blonde who would put up or shut up. He was a man's man and a woman's fantasy.

On film, they were like cats in heat—fiery lovers and equally fierce foes. They were never quite aware of how deep their feelings ran, at least until the last reel. Together, Harlow and Gable brought sizzle to the screen and millions of dollars to MGM. Audiences adored them.

Both actors were on the verge of becoming major stars in 1931, when they were cast with top-billed Wallace Beery in *The Secret Six*. Harlow was given fourth billing, and Gable sixth. Yet, even in their minor roles, they stood out among the bootleg crowd in this film.

MGM bought Harlow's contract from Howard Hughes for $60,000 and gave Gable a long-term contract. Yet, despite this good fortune, Gable didn't think he was going to last in Hollywood. Over dinner one night with actor Ralph Bellamy, Gable said: "I just got paid eleven thousand dollars for playing a heavy in a Bill

Opposite:
Lust in the *Red Dust* with Jean Harlow and Clark Gable in a classic clinch.

Harlow and Gable appeared together for the first time in *The Secret Six*, a hardboiled gangster movie.

27

Though they didn't have the leading roles in *The Secret Six*,
Harlow and Gable made their mark as rising stars. Clearly, they played well together.

Boyd western. Eleven thousand dollars—no actor's worth that! I've got myself a room at the Castle Argyle up at the head of Vine Street; I've bought a second-hand Ford. But I'm not buying anything you can't put on the Santa Fe Chief because this isn't going to last."

He was born William Clark Gable in Cadiz, Ohio, in 1901, and got into movies through his work as a stagehand. He appeared in a few silent films and then went back to the theater. His friend Lionel Barrymore got him a screen test, which was rejected at both MGM and Warner Brothers. But the advent of talkies was priming Hollywood for actors with both stage experience and strong voices. In 1931 producer Irving Thalberg relented, and gave Gable a two-year contract with MGM for $350 a week, casting him as a heavy in supporting roles. He made three films with Joan Crawford, which galvanized his ever-growing legion of fans. His image as a sex symbol was further enhanced when he was cast in the first of several risqué movies with Jean Harlow.

By then, Harlow was commanding $1,200 a week at MGM. Born Harlean Carpenter in Kansas City, Missouri, in 1911, she arrived in Hollywood at the age of sixteen, after a disastrous first marriage. She appeared in minor roles until Howard Hughes starred her in *Hell's Angels* in 1930. The movie was a hit, and Harlow was loaned out several times, most notably to Frank Capra in 1931 for *Platinum Blonde*, a film that took advantage of the star's distinctive hair color. She quickly became known as "The Platinum Blonde" and "The Blonde Bombshell."

Harlow would probably have been the first to admit she had little real acting talent. Her two acting modes were screeching and sulking, but she was startlingly sexual. She never wore underwear, which was readily apparent through her signature white satin gowns. She oozed sexuality and seemed to want sex as much as any man, which was both titillating and liberating for her time. She became one of the most photographed stars in fan magazines, and her fan mail increased daily by hundreds of letters.

Part of Harlow's appeal was her honesty. She never hid who she was, never put on airs. In *Red Dust* she's stranded on Gable's rubber plantation after her steamship breaks down. Explaining why she's so restless after dinner, she says: "Guess I'm not used to sleeping nights."

The famous rain barrel bath scene from *Red Dust* caused a sensation when Harlow's then-husband, Paul Bern, fought with her about wearing a swimsuit for the shot. She refused to put one on, and when Bern committed suicide only days later, the gossips had a field day.

Despite her faults as an actress, Harlow had a real flair for comedy, as did Gable. And their scripts were tailor-made. According to writer John Lee Mahin: "When I'd write things like *Red Dust* I'd give the girl the cracks because Gable was funniest when he reacted. And he'd say, 'Gees, John, those lines are not particularly funny.' I'd tell him, 'But your reaction when we cut to you—that's the funny thing. The audience doesn't really start to laugh—doesn't get it—until that big kisser of yours comes on and you're terribly uncomfortable or sore.' Clark accepted that."

The ads for *Red Dust* proclaimed: "They were born to co-star!" and the movie was a smash, despite the notoriety it garnered when, during filming, Harlow's husband of two months, movie executive Paul Bern, committed suicide by shooting himself in the head. It

was well known they had quarreled during Harlow's famous bath scene in a rain barrel. (She had refused to wear any kind of bathing suit.) Bern's cryptic suicide note was highly publicized. "Dearest Dear," he wrote, "Unfortunately, this is the only way to make good the frightful wrong I have done you and to wipe out my abject humiliation. Paul. You understand that last night was only a comedy."

It was later revealed that Bern was impotent, but at the time many fans thought the suicide had been caused, at least in part, by Gable's attraction to Harlow.

No one has ever verified whether Harlow and Gable actually were lovers. Aside from the scandalous gossip, most people who were close to the couple claim they were not intimate in real life. But everyone agrees Harlow and Gable understood each other and knew how to play their respective screen types. Photographer Clarence Bull reported that when the pair posed for publicity pictures they'd "kid around and wrestle until I'd say, 'Let's heat up the negative.' And they almost burned it clear through. I've never seen two actors make love so convincingly without being in love. How they enjoyed those embraces. And the jokes and the laughter."

Their next picture together, *Hold Your Man*, was written by Anita Loos expressly for them. In it the wise-cracks fly fast and furiously. Playing a petty crook, Gable meets Harlow after he breaks into her apartment. Once again, she's taking a bath. She comes out of the bathroom, and when the police arrive to search the place, Gable gets in the tub wearing his pants. Later, Harlow gives him a robe while she attempts to dry his pants. "Say, this is a man's robe!" he exclaims. "You don't say?" she counters. "Ain't you a bright little thing?"

He interrupts her ironing: "That reminds me. I left something in my pants pocket. Say, listen, I had two tens when I come in here. What could've happened to the other one?" Harlow glances at him over her shoulder. "That must be awful hard for you to figure out," she quips. There's a note of admiration in Gable's voice when he concedes: "Okay, you got it coming to you."

Opposite:
"You talk too much but you're a cute little trick at that," Gable says to Harlow in *Red Dust*.

Later in this film, Harlow performs jungle surgery on Gable after he's shot by the jilted Mary Astor.

Two hustlers with hearts of gold, Gable and Harlow meet "cute" when he breaks into her bathroom to escape the cops in *Hold Your Man* (left). He then jumps in the tub wearing his pants, which he automatically assumes she'll iron for him later (right).

He decides to turn on the charm, but they are two of a kind, and he doesn't fool her for a moment. "Even your smile is crooked," she comments. When he asks if she objects, she only grins and says, "Not at all. It's your mouth. You can do what you want with it." In the game of cat and mouse, Harlow and Gable turn somersaults as the pursuer and the willingly pursued.

Hold Your Man opened at the Capitol Theater in New York on June 30, 1933. *Variety* proclaimed:

"(There's) nothing wrong with the ethics of the situation in which both principal characters start as unworthy, for it is the honest love they find in each other that works out their regeneration. That outline ought to be censor-proof."

The film was a hit, like most of Harlow's movies, which averaged sales of between ten and fifteen million adult theater tickets. Profits for MGM on Harlow-Gable movies soared because, although both were star

Opposite:
Shooting a love scene from *Hold Your Man* with director Sam Wood (top) that was eventually cut from the film. The often-photographed couple had a winning appeal that is evident in this MGM publicity still (bottom).

attractions, they were only receiving salaries of good feature players.

In 1933, about a year after Paul Bern's suicide, Harlow married Harold Rosson, a distinguished cameraman who had photographed her in *Red Dust*. The marriage lasted less than a year, and she started seeing a lot of her sometime costar William Powell.

Then, MGM reassembled the cast from *The Secret Six* for *China Seas*. Gable's top billing reflected his new status. Harlow's name followed, and then Wallace Beery's. The three stars insured box-office success, as did Harlow's loose-topped, tight-bottomed gown, which created a sensation.

Here, she again plays Gable's mistress, wearing an armload of bangles that jangle throughout the movie. He plays the captain of the ship, and isn't exactly happy when she buys a ticket to accompany him to Hong Kong. Although he allows her to stay on board, he's clear about the nature of their relationship. "You and I are friends," Gable reminds Harlow. "We've had a lot of fun together. As far as I'm concerned, you're the number one girl in the archipelago. But I don't remember making any vows to you, nor do I recall asking for any."

Then, classy Rosalind Russell boards the ship and rekindles an old love affair with Gable. A distraught Harlow aids Beery in pirating the boat, then explains why she has double-crossed Gable: "When a woman can love a man right down to his fingertips, she can hate him just the same."

During the filming of *China Seas* Gable refused to allow a double for his action shots, insisting on doing all his own stunts, even for a dangerous scene in which he

Opposite:
Gable plays a dashing but bullheaded skipper, and Harlow his sometime girlfriend in *China Seas*.
Right:
He's a hard drinker with Harlow (top) but looks more presentable (center) around bluebloods Rosalind Russell and C. Aubrey Smith. The movie was a smash hit at the box office (bottom), with MGM promoting their three-star triumph. In most of their films together, Gable and Harlow played compatible low-lifes, and audiences loved them. Unlike foreign idols such as Valentino, sexy Clark Gable was non-threatening to men. And Harlow was the kind of woman you might see at the five-and-dime. According to her biographer, Irving Shulman: "Women reproved (Harlow) for behaving wickedly with her body, but loved her for not being wicked in mind."

Above:
Harlow changes stride in *Wife vs. Secretary*, where she plays a working girl with the smarts to assist Gable in a top-secret business deal. For once, he appreciates her for her brains.
Opposite:
Wife meets secretary in *Wife vs. Secretary*. As Gable's spouse, Myrna Loy holds back her jealousy, for the moment at least, when Harlow arrives at their apartment.

had to harness a runaway steamroller to the deck of the ship. A *Times* reviewer wrote: "It is a role which demands vigor, an infectious, devil-may-care philosophy and the stinging passion of distempered blood, and while Gable has displayed these qualities before, it is one of his most convincing portrayals." His legend as star material was growing.

So was Harlow's. In August 1933, *Time* called her "the foremost U.S. embodiment of sex appeal." By this point in her career, Harlow had become frustrated at

continually being cast as the platinum floozy with an eighteen-karat heart. She was eager to prove herself, and therefore happy when she was cast with Gable and Myrna Loy in *Wife vs. Secretary*. Although the story is rather trite, Harlow has a change-of-pace role in it. She plays Gable's smart, sassy, and charming secretary. More toned down here than in any other movie she made with Gable, she doesn't screech, scream, or throw tantrums. She doesn't slap anyone or get slapped herself. Her hair is darker, her makeup is softer, her jewelry is minimal, and she dresses in tailored suits. She even appears to be wearing underwear.

The plot is as predictable as the title of the movie indicates. Gable and Loy are rich, successful, and very much in love. "Happy?" Gable asks Loy. "I don't know," she replies. "You've never shown me anything other." Meanwhile, Gable and Harlow are working overtime on a takeover deal so secret that even Loy doesn't know about it. So Loy doesn't understand why Harlow flies down to Havana to work with Gable. When Loy calls Gable's hotel room at 2 A.M., Harlow answers the phone. Gable rushes back to New York, but it's too late. Loy wants a divorce.

In the surprise ending Harlow delivered her dialogue with a maturity she had rarely displayed before. She proved she could indeed act if given intelligent material. In this telling scene Harlow also revealed the essence of her screen character and the foundation of her screen relationship with Gable throughout their collaboration.

Admittedly, she's a "bad girl" in the eyes of some, but she's no dummy. She's crazy about him, as she suspects every woman would be. If the opportunity presents itself to make a play for him, she's going to take it. Her intentions are honorable in that she's always honest about them. In her way, Harlow is always guileless. Under all the flash and glitter, beneath the platinum and the satin, Harlow is vulnerable—as tough as nails on the outside, cotton candy on the inside. In *China Seas*, she's willing to give up Gable if he loves Russell, and she'll step aside in *Red Dust* if Gable prefers Mary Astor.

In *Wife vs. Secretary*, Harlow gives Loy fair warning of her intentions. When Harlow discovers Loy is sailing for Europe, she rushes to the ship. Loy doesn't want to speak with Harlow, thinking she knows exactly what Harlow is going to say.

LOY: My husband loves me. He's innocent. You want me to go back to him. What else?
HARLOW: But I don't want you to go back to him. I hope he never sees you again.
LOY: You're frank about it, anyway. You'd really better go.
HARLOW: If you leave him now, you'll never get him back.
LOY: Yes, it's occurred to me.
HARLOW: He's going to be lonely. His life won't end with you, you know, and when the rebound sets in, he's going to turn to the woman nearest him, and you know who it'll be.
LOY: I'm sure I do.
HARLOW: Tomorrow he's taking me to Bermuda, as a friend, but it won't go on like this. Pretty soon he'll want to buy me things. That's how it always starts, and then it will be too late, because if he ever turns to me, I won't turn away. . . . I'll take him second best but he'll be fairly happy. Not as happy as he was, not as happy as you could make him, but as happy as anybody else could make him. You're still going?
LOY: Yes.
HARLOW: You're a fool, for which I'm grateful.

The film was surely a high point in Harlow's career. Her personal life was also going well. William Powell gave her a 150-carat star sapphire ring as a Christmas present. The papers reported it as an unofficial engagement ring costing $20,000. At the same time, Gable was seeing Carole Lombard, who had divorced William Powell.

This was Hollywood divorce team tag at its most bizarre. Powell and Lombard had been married in 1931, when he was thirty-eight years of age and she was twenty-two. (He had divorced his wife of ten years in order to marry Lombard.) The Lombard-Powell marriage dissolved in 1933, but they remained great friends. In fact, because they were seen together so much, the gossip columnists often speculated they would remarry.

In 1935, Gable was shooting *Call of the Wild* with Loretta Young. The two were rumored to be in the midst of a torrid love affair that interfered with the location filming. After the production wrapped, Young disappeared for many months, returning to Hollywood with an infant child in tow. She claimed she had adopted the

Jean Harlow died only a short time after shooting this
scene with Gable in *Saratoga*. It was rumored that the flowers at her funeral
cost $25,000, which was more than her entire estate was worth after her
debts had been paid.

orphan, but rumors persisted that Gable had fathered the child. Indeed, Young once said, "I think every woman he ever met was in love with him."

Rumors of various women—including journalist Adela Rogers St. John, Gable's close friend for many years—secretly bearing his love child would repeatedly crop up in Hollywood. When Merv Griffin questioned St. John about this during a broadcast in March 1975, she replied: "What woman would deny Clark Gable was the father of her child?"

Gable was, in fact, a notorious womanizer. At least until he met his match in Carole Lombard. They met in 1932 while filming *No Man of Her Own,* but didn't begin to date seriously until 1936, when Powell and Harlow were a hot item. Supposedly, the foursome were great chums, even though Lombard suspected Harlow and Gable had once been lovers, a circumstance to which Gable would never admit.

During this happy period, shooting began for Harlow's last film, *Saratoga.* On May 29, 1937, one month into production, Gable and Harlow shot a scene calling for him to carry her to the couch and then drop her. But as Gable lifted her he noticed she was in a cold sweat, even under the white-hot lights. She felt limp in his arms. He gently placed her down, and told the director she was ill. Harlow protested but then fainted.

She was revived with smelling salts and taken home. Before leaving, she stopped on the set of *Double Wedding* to tell Powell she was breaking their lunch date. It was the last time he saw her alive.

Harlow died on June 7, 1937, at the age of twenty-six. The cause of her death remains something of a mystery. Some say she died of an acute gall bladder infection and kidney failure, and others claim she was the victim of cerebral edema following uremic poisoning. Whatever the cause, her untimely passing caused a sensation.

"The news of Harlow's death spread so quickly that Carole Lombard told Gable the Associated Press must have secretly taped a wire to the actress's wrist so they'd know the moment her pulse stopped," writes author Warren Harris. "Not since Rudolph Valentino died of a perforated ulcer in 1926 had one of Hollywood's great sex symbols succumbed at the height of fame and popularity. With 88 million Ameri-cans worshipping in movie cathedrals every week, it was a tragedy epic enough to sweep even the honeymoon of the Duke and Duchess of Windsor out of the headlines."

When Harlow died, she still had several days of shooting left on *Saratoga,* and at first MGM announced they would close down production and reshoot the whole film with another actress. An editorial in the *Los Angeles Examiner* implored Mayer to shoot the final scenes with a double: "Jean Harlow was an artist and did her work up to the time she was called . . . that work should not be disregarded."

Ultimately, Harlow's remaining scenes were filmed in long shot with a double. Gable was visibly shaken. "I feel like I've been holding a ghost in my arms all day," he complained to Lombard.

Saratoga was a box-office success, partly because of the publicity generated by Harlow's death. Audiences were eager to see her last performance and to guess which scenes featured her double. As in all the movies Harlow and Gable made together, *Saratoga* shows their rapport. He loved to joke with her—both on screen and off—and she is said to have been very clever with a phrase. She's known for such Harlowisms as: "Usually the self-made man quits too soon" and "A woman's mind should always be clean—she changes it often enough."

Gable's love scenes with Harlow were as sexy as any he ever played. She appeared to urge him on in a way no one else would have dared to, though she did it in fun. She greatly enhanced his screen image as a macho man who eventually does right by the woman who loves him. And, partly because of the success of her pictures with Gable, Harlow became one of the first American sex symbols. Most of those who came after her—Marilyn Monroe, Lana Turner, Kim Novak, even Madonna—took their cue from Harlow. All were blonde, buxom, and blatantly sexual. Harlow set the mold. It has yet to be broken.

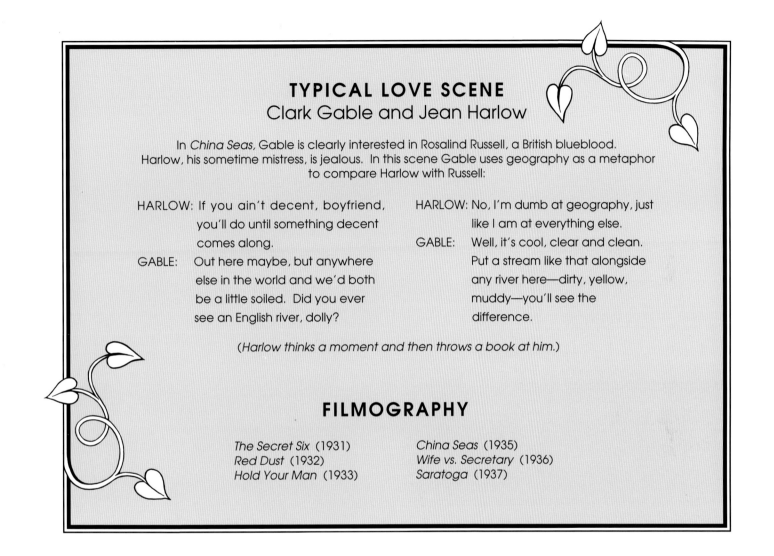

TYPICAL LOVE SCENE
Clark Gable and Jean Harlow

In *China Seas,* Gable is clearly interested in Rosalind Russell, a British blueblood.
Harlow, his sometime mistress, is jealous. In this scene Gable uses geography as a metaphor
to compare Harlow with Russell:

HARLOW: If you ain't decent, boyfriend, you'll do until something decent comes along.

GABLE: Out here maybe, but anywhere else in the world and we'd both be a little soiled. Did you ever see an English river, dolly?

HARLOW: No, I'm dumb at geography, just like I am at everything else.

GABLE: Well, it's cool, clear and clean. Put a stream like that alongside any river here—dirty, yellow, muddy—you'll see the difference.

(Harlow thinks a moment and then throws a book at him.)

FILMOGRAPHY

The Secret Six (1931)
Red Dust (1932)
Hold Your Man (1933)

China Seas (1935)
Wife vs. Secretary (1936)
Saratoga (1937)

glamour
CRAWFORD & GABLE

CRAWFORD: I saw your face in the wings;
made me feel I was doing everything wrong.

GABLE: I got that kind of face.

DANCING LADY (1933)

In the movies, Jean Harlow always had to compete for Clark Gable's affections. Her rivals were sophisticates and bluebloods, as played by Mary Astor in *Red Dust*, Rosalind Russell in *China Seas*, and Myrna Loy in *Wife vs. Secretary*. Not so with Joan Crawford. In fact, in five out of the eight movies they made together, Gable won Crawford from another man. Yet, unlike the battles Harlow waged to win Gable, these were never real rivalries. In all their movies, Gable and Crawford were meant to be together from the first reel. Gable may have sizzled with Harlow, but he smoldered with love for Crawford.

Louis B. Mayer called Joan Crawford the first MGM "creation." Pulled from the ranks of the chorus girls, she was fashioned into a star, with glamour as her trademark. In almost every movie Crawford made, she appeared at least once in an evening gown, sometimes under the most improbable conditions. In *Love on the Run*, she and Gable steal a truck, which is fortunately carrying evening gowns, to make their getaway. In a penal colony on a deserted island in *Strange Cargo*, Crawford wears a beaded gown to sing in a seedy bar.

Gable, for his part, was a symbol of rugged manhood. He looked just as good in a torn T-shirt as he did in a tux. He was the king of the working class. Gable didn't need fancy clothes or high-class dialogue. He needed only his crooked smile to attract Crawford.

Opposite:
Publicity still from *Love on the Run*, the seventh and next-to-last film featuring Joan Crawford and Clark Gable. In all of their films together, she was the epitome of Hollywood glamour, and he symbolized rugged manhood. Even though many of their films were less than major hits, with the right script they were capable of making movie magic.

The two had a lot in common; both were among the most durable stars in Hollywood. Though they each suffered various highs and lows in their careers, both continued working until their deaths.

Crawford was a major star when she first appeared with Gable. In 1937, *Life* magazine said: "It is an axiom in Hollywood that movie favorites are usually created by women. Joan Crawford's public is predominately female, predominately lowbrow. A former shopgirl herself, she has risen to stardom as the Shopgirl's Dream." Crawford's screen image was always that of the working girl who made good, and women of the '30s and '40s identified with her. "Whatever role she played, (her) character kept pace with any masculine rival on the screen," writes Crawford's biographer, Jane Ellen Wayne. "Gable complemented her best because his role was to dodge or dominate dames. Moviegoers' subconscious identification with this image is one reason why Crawford's fans did not abandon her. Letters with the same theme poured in to MGM: 'Dear Joan, if you can do it, so can I.'"

She was born Lucille Fay Le Sueur, in 1904, in San Antonio, Texas. Nicknamed Billie Cassin (after her stepfather), the twenty-one-year-old arrived in Hollywood in 1925, and began a lifelong obsession with reinventing herself. Her new name was the result of an MGM-sponsored contest in *Movie Weekly*. She never abandoned the fans who christened her, personally answering all her fan letters in longhand.

Crawford graduated from bit parts to leads in lesser films, and was put to work in every type of movie: comedies, melodramas, thrillers, romancers, westerns, and jazz-age silents. She worked hard and learned from everyone, making friends with cast and crew as she studied lighting, camera angles, makeup, set design, and costuming. She was a workhorse, a go-getter, and a movie queen before the term had even been coined.

After working all day at MGM, she would dance away the night, perfecting a wild Charleston. F. Scott Fitzgerald once wrote: "Joan Crawford is doubtless the best example of the flapper, the girl you see at smart nightclubs, gowned to the apex of sophistication, toying with iced glasses with a remote, faintly bitter expression, dancing deliciously, laughing a great deal, with wide, hurt eyes."

She dated in the right places and never appeared in public without looking every inch a star. Paul Bern numbered among her numerous escorts for several years before he married Jean Harlow. Bern took Crawford to dinner parties and premieres. He helped advance her career, advising her to tone down her flapper image, to stop chewing gum, and to hire a drama coach. Under Bern's guidance, Crawford flourished at MGM and was receiving top billing when, in 1931, Gable was assigned to work with her in *Dance, Fools, Dance*.

Gable had played minor gangster roles, but he was hardly considered a leading man at the time. From all reports he was nervous about appearing with Crawford. "She was a star and knew the ropes in pictures," he told a reporter. "I was afraid she'd laugh behind my back."

Though Gable only appears in a few scenes, he is convincing as a gangster who lures Crawford's brother into killing a reporter. And he made a lasting impression on Crawford, who later said that when she first met him "it was like an electric current went right through my whole body. There was a thing that went through the two of us like dynamite. . . . In the one scene where he grabbed me and threatened the life of my brother, his nearness had such an impact, my knees buckled. If he hadn't held me by both shoulders, I'd have dropped."

Their attraction for each other was the start of what one observer called "the affair that nearly burned Hollywood down." At the time, Crawford was married to Douglas Fairbanks, Jr., son of Douglas Fairbanks, Sr., and step-son of Mary Pickford. From Pickfair, their residence, the Fairbankses presided like Hollywood royalty. The affair between Crawford and Gable generated nonstop gossip in Hollywood, and Mayer didn't approve. Crawford was a major star, and Gable was a lowly contract player. Mayer warned him to stay

In their first film, *Dance, Fools, Dance*, Gable makes a play for Crawford, a down-on-her-luck heiress. He only appears in a few scenes, but he is totally convincing as a bad guy (above). Gangster Gable man-handles Crawford (right) so she can't warn her brother that Earle Foxe is about to pounce.

away from her and, not knowing what to do, he married socialite Rhea Langham in March 1931.

It was his second marriage. Both his wives were much older than Gable: Josephine Dillon by twelve years, Langham by fourteen. They helped promote his career and take care of him. Some critics have attributed Gable's attraction to older women to the fact that his own mother, an epileptic, had died nine months after giving birth to him.

Gable was also a ladies' man. In addition to his numerous affairs, he was known to frequent the establishment of a famous Hollywood madam. A friend once asked him why he paid for sex when so many other, more desirable women were willing to be his for the asking. He answered: "Because with one of those floozies, I don't have to pretend that I'm Clark Gable."

Crawford claimed that she and Gable had had a thirty-year love affair. When asked why they never married, Crawford replied: "We were too much alike to make a go of it. Bless L. B. Mayer for stopping us. We would have destroyed a wonderful relationship that lasted until he died." She also told writer Roy Newquist: "Few people understood my relationship with Clark. We taught each other how to laugh at ourselves. . . . Clark was a wonderful man. Very simple, actually, pretty much the way he's been painted. He was more of a womanizer than the studio wanted to admit, but any relationship he entered into was honest—no false hopes. He outgrew his first two wives, and he felt terribly sorry about the breakups."

In 1931 Crawford and Gable made their second film, *Laughing Sinners*. In it, she plays a reckless dance-hall girl who is abandoned by her boyfriend, a traveling salesman. Despondent, she attempts to jump off a bridge and is rescued by Gable, a Salvation Army volunteer. He sets Crawford on the road to living for others. She has a relapse when her boyfriend returns, but Gable puts her straight.

The film originally previewed as *Complete Surrender*, but a chilly audience reaction convinced producer Irving Thalberg to recut it. The movie bombed anyway. However, Thalberg detected the chemistry between Crawford and Gable, and instructed the story department to find a script for them. Writer Frances Marion was told to tailor Gable's screen character to this specific formula: "He's tough, uneducated, got a

Playing against type in *Laughing Sinners*, Gable's a recruiting do-gooder for the Salvation Army who rescues Crawford from a life of sin. "Living for others makes you forget yourself," he tells her. She believes him until her married boyfriend hits town.

hell of a temper, can fight his weight in wildcats . . . with sex that drives women crazy."

Though many critics argued that Gable did not display real acting talent, especially in his early films, it didn't seem to matter to his fans. He had a way about him that was both manly and magnetic. "He pushed women around, traded insults with them, pinched their behinds; he pretended to despise them, while secretly adoring," writes David Shipman. The formula worked, and Crawford helped transform him into a screen idol, adding glamour and romance to his image.

Their next, and probably their best, film together was *Possessed* (1931). (Crawford filmed another movie with the same title in 1947). She asked that Gable be her

Crawford realizes there's only one trap that can ruin a woman: falling in love with a man like Gable.

Ironically, Crawford was having the same problem in real life. "I knew I was falling into a trap I warned young girls about—not to fall in love with leading men or take romantic scenes to heart," she later said. "Leave the set and forget about it because that marvelous feeling would pass. Boy, I had to eat those words, but they tasted very sweet. . . . Our relationship was physical, but it went beyond that. . . . We were nobodies transformed into somebodies by Hollywood. We were unhappily married to people who tried to change us. . . . Clark was the first damned friend I could talk to in Hollywood. . . . When we first became involved, he told me it wasn't his thing to get involved with a married woman. I was the exception. We were both in and out of affairs, marriages, and divorces all the time, but we survived them all."

Perhaps *Possessed* was so successful because, by then, Crawford and Gable were at the height of their love affair. In any case, the film was well received. *Photoplay* wrote: "You really don't care if the story is old and some of the lines a little shopworn. For the Gable boy and the Crawford girl make you believe it. . . . It's the best work Joan Crawford has done since *Paid* and Clark Gable—he's everybody's big moment. If Joan weren't so good, he'd have the picture."

Above and right:
In *Dancing Lady* Crawford's an aspiring hoofer, and Gable's a tough producer. ("Compared to him, an elephant's skin is tissue paper.") She manages to melt his heart by the fade-out. In real life, though, Gable lost her to costar Franchot Tone, who became Crawford's second husband after they worked together on this movie.

costar for this predictable vehicle, in which she plays a small-town factory worker yearning for bigger things. In one early scene, Crawford stands at a railroad crossing and stares longingly into a passing train, sighing with envy as each slow-moving car reveals yet another glimpse of the high life. Crawford dumps her hip boyfriend and heads for New York, where she meets fabulously wealthy Gable. She tells him she's looking for a rich man; he's impressed with her honesty and her legs.

She becomes his mistress. He sets her up in an art-deco apartment and introduces her to his friends as a divorced woman, living on alimony, to avoid any gossip. He showers her with expensive gifts and teaches her everything she needs to know about fine wines, gourmet foods, and entertaining in high society.

But even though he loves and respects her, he refuses to marry her. As ever, smiling through her tears,

Pool play in *Chained*. Crawford is caught in a love triangle between Gable and Otto Kruger. Guess who wins her heart in the last scene?

Gable made twelve pictures in 1931 (three with Crawford), and was earning a fortune for MGM, but Mayer still considered his popularity a fad. According to Charles Samuels, Gable's biographer, MGM "kept on insisting that Gable was a freak box-office attraction who would disappear once the public was tired of gangster pictures." Mayer called Gable "a gigolo with brass knuckles."

Despite Gable's protests, Mayer cast him opposite Crawford in *Dancing Lady* in 1933. Crawford needed a hit. Her two previous films, *Rain* (for which she was loaned to United Artists) and *Today We Live*, had flopped at the box office, and it was hoped a Crawford-Gable vehicle would give a much-needed boost to her career. In *Dancing Lady*, Gable plays a Broadway producer who makes Crawford a star and then steals her away from playboy Franchot Tone.

The movie was a big hit. Crawford's career was back on track, but Gable was not nearly as happy about the project and complained bitterly to Mayer. He was upset with constantly having to pay consort to studio queens and was fed up with second billing. Perhaps his anger was fueled by the love affair that developed between Crawford and Tone during *Dancing Lady*. Whatever his reasons, Gable refused to work. He entered the hospital after the film

wrapped, and Mayer suspended him for two months. Then, Mayer loaned Gable out to Frank Capra at the far-from-prestigious Columbia Pictures for a film called *It Happened One Night*. This was supposed to be punishment, but Gable parlayed the role into an Oscar.

In 1934 Gable returned to MGM to film *Chained*, a shipboard soap opera with Crawford walking both sides of the bad-girl street. As a single woman, she chases a married man (Otto Kruger). As a married woman, she chases a single man (Gable). The simplistic plot hardly mattered. By then, the reputation of Gable and Crawford as a screen couple almost guaranteed their movie would be a hit. As the *New York Times* said: "So long as Miss Crawford and Mr. Gable are in a picture, it is as inevitable as the coming of night that the characters they impersonate will not be disappointing in the end. Miss Crawford gives a facile performance, and Mr. Gable is as ingratiating as ever."

The team was less successful when cast in screwball comedies. Mayer wanted to capitalize on the success of *It Happened One Night*, so he assigned Crawford and Gable to *Forsaking All Others*, in which Crawford's only memorable line is: "Don't be silly, I'm not going to faint. I'm not the type." The movie was received with minimal enthusiasm. MGM made a second attempt with *Love on the Run*, in which the forced antagonism runs to lines such as: "You're something that flies out of the jar when they take the lid off." Neither star was happy about these vehicles, as they knew screwball comedy was not their forte. Mayer finally agreed. In 1940, after two failures, they were paired together for the last time in *Strange Cargo*, a bizarre melodrama with religious overtones.

As always, in this film Gable and Crawford are antagonists, but here they go at each other with unprecedented bitterness. Their dialogue is biting, and they double-cross each other whenever possible. Yet their mutual attraction is undeniable. "You got class kid, or is it because I haven't seen a woman lately?" Gable wonders. (He's been imprisoned in a penal colony for several years.) "I don't know what you'll look like tomorrow, but tonight you're the best looking thing I've ever seen," he tells her after his escape.

She's too tough to be insulted and too ruthless not to turn him over to the cops. "You outsmarted me," he says. "That's what happens when smart people get together. One of them comes out ahead," she comments.

Even Crawford's tender moments with Gable are iced with antagonism. "Who's a rat, baby?" he asks. "You are," she says. He smirks, "But I'll do anyway." Scenes such as this one clearly show that Gable's effect on women virtually made his career. Crawford defined his appeal in this way: "He knew where he was the minute he looked at a woman. He knew what he would get back from that woman if he gave her the right look; he'd seen that reaction on the screen too often not to know. And he loved it if there was a new woman around and he could walk into a room and hear her sigh. He didn't even have to hear—he could see."

Gable's friend, Howard Strickling, an MGM publicity man, confirmed that Gable approached women in real social situations the same way he did on screen: "The first thing he always did, you know, he'd look her over. She'd know damn well that he was sizing her up head to foot. And he was looking at her eyes and he was looking at her lips, you know, and she'd know damn well that he was sizing her up while he was squinting at her, and she'd wonder what this guy was thinking about, you know. He'd ask a lot of questions . . . and he'd have a few laughs with her. If he sensed she didn't respond the way he expected, he might clam up a bit. But mostly, they responded." Women dropped like flies at his feet. Ursula Theiss, who was married to Robert Taylor, once said: "He made you feel twice the woman you thought you were."

On the screen Gable was charming, even when he was being a rat. He would sweep Crawford into his arms and, though she might protest for a moment, she was soon overcome. There was a method to Gable's screen kisses. His biographer Lyn Tornabene writes that "the kisses still seem convincing today, but they don't steam by any current standards because the Hays Office wouldn't let them. Though the Motion Picture Production Code formulated in 1930 by the Association of Motion Picture Producers didn't specifically prohibit open-mouthed kissing until it (the code) was revised in (1934), directors knew that a kiss scene was subject to cutting if either kisser's lips were even faintly parted. Gable's kisses, throughout his career, were so tight-lipped audiences could well have wondered whether he was afraid his teeth would fall out. He probably was conscious of this himself, because he developed a

Above and opposite:
In *Forsaking All Others* Crawford almost marries Robert Montgomery before Gable confesses that he has loved her for twenty years. The screwball comedy is as dull as dishwater, but the love scenes always sizzle.

technique—obvious in many of his films—that involved holding his partner and subtly turning her away from the camera so that their kiss wasn't seen head-on."

The reputation that made Gable a star plagued him outside the movie theater. In the spring of 1937, a woman named Violet Norton claimed he had fathered her daughter, resulting in a famous paternity suit and blackmail scandal. In court, Gable testified about his relationship with Franz Dorfler, which had been the first serious affair of his life. The attorney asked what happened after Gable had thrown over Dorfler. "What makes you think I threw her over?" asked Gable. "You

Opposite:
Even though *Forsaking All Others* flopped at the box office, L. B. Mayer cast Gable and Crawford in another screwball comedy, *Love on the Run*. When it, too, proved disastrous, MGM finally realized that audiences weren't prepared to laugh at any movie featuring these two superstars, who took their romance seriously both on screen and off.

must have. No one ever heard of a girl walking out on Clark Gable." Even in a court of law, he was everybody's fantasy of his screen persona.

Despite his lawsuits (he was acquitted in the Norton case), Gable's personal life in the late 1930s was at its most satisfying because of Carole Lombard, who clearly was the love of his life. They married, bought a ranch, and settled down to domestic bliss. Though very popular in her own right, Lombard began turning down films in order to spend more time as Mrs. Clark Gable. By all accounts, it was a very successful marriage. Then, on January 16, 1942, less than three years after the wedding, Lombard died in a plane crash as she was returning from a tour to promote war bonds. Joan Crawford remembered that "Clark came to me that night. He was drunk and he cried. There was nothing I could say. Nothing meant anything to him anymore. . . . He was never the same anymore."

At the time of her death, Lombard had been scheduled by Columbia to star in *They All Kissed the Bride*. Crawford volunteered to replace Lombard and donated her salary of $125,000 to the Red Cross. (When Crawford's agent tried to take his ten-percent commission, she fired him.) Hollywood gossips dredged up stories of the former affair between Gable and Crawford and claimed that she was trying to get him back. People who knew Crawford said that she always regretted not having married him when he proposed in the early 1930s.

Despondent with grief over the loss of Lombard, Gable enlisted during the war. His marriage eight years later to Lady Sylvia Ashley only lasted a year and a half. His fifth and last wedding took place in July 1955, when he was fifty-four and Kay Williams Spreckels was thirty-nine. It was a peaceful, happy union, which lasted until his death on November 16, 1960. His only son was born four months later.

Crawford was devastated when Gable died. "Part of me went with him. He knew more about me than anyone else," she said. By that time, her career was in sharp decline, as there weren't many roles available for aging movie queens. This is probably why she agreed in the early 1960s to work in *What Ever Happened to Baby Jane?* with Bette Davis. The two old war-horses were enough to draw crowds to the theaters, and Crawford did several other horror films.

Crawford married four times. Her first three husbands were all actors (Douglas Fairbanks, Jr., Franchot Tone, and Philip Terry), and each of those marriages lasted four years. In 1956, she married the chairman of the board of Pepsi-Cola, Alfred Steele, and embarked on a second career as spokesperson for that soft drink. Though Steele died in 1959, Crawford continued to work with the corporation. She died in 1977.

Crawford once explained her philosophy about relationships like this: "When a love affair begins, it's like a new dress. It may be your favorite. There's an accident. You tear it. You love it, so you patch it—cleverly, daintily—so that no one can see it. Yet *you* know you have patched it. The next time, perhaps, you burn it. Again you patch it and conceal it, but you know it is no longer perfect. Finally, after much patching and mending you can no longer pretend, even to yourself, that the dress is 'as good as new.' You may still think it is the prettiest dress in your wardrobe, but it is patched beyond wearing.

"The only thing to do, then, is to be brave and discard it! Bury the shreds in the prison of your heart as you bury the shreds of your dress in your mending basket. Remember only its first beauty, when it was new and glittering and attractive!" How fitting that the shop girl who had made good would use clothing as a metaphor for love.

In the early 1970s, Crawford was asked by David Frost on a national broadcast to name Hollywood's most exciting actor. Without a moment's hesitation she named Gable. "Why Gable?" asked Frost. "Because he had balls," declared Crawford. Her answer was bleeped off the air.

Overleaf:
**Two tough cookies in *Strange Cargo*.
"You hit hard, baby, so you love hard," observes Gable after Crawford whacks him in the head, which for this film couple was little more than foreplay.**

TYPICAL LOVE SCENE
Joan Crawford and Clark Gable

In *Strange Cargo* Crawford turns Gable, an escaped convict, over to the law
and then is forced to leave the penal colony. She has no money for the boat home,
so she hitches a ride with bad guy Marfeu, who takes her to the mining camp
where he lives. Meanwhile, Gable escapes and breaks into their cabin.
He demands food, and she dumps a can of something into a frying pan.
Gable takes a bite and glares at Crawford:

GABLE: Garbage—but good enough for a man when he's starving—so you'll do, too,
      baby.
CRAWFORD: Thanks.
GABLE: This is no time to be particular. Funny, a man should want something he's got
      no use for, and I got no use for you. You know that, don't you?
CRAWFORD: And how much do you think I think of you?
GABLE: How much?
CRAWFORD: So much that if you ever made the mistake of turning your back on me,
      I'd. . . .
GABLE: You'd run a knife into it? You ain't got that kind of stuff, sweetheart. There they
      are . . . (*He tosses the knives at her*) but you won't use them. Takes something
      to gamble that way, something that a cheap dame hasn't got and you're
      cheap. If you'd waited back there and run the scissors into me when I wasn't
      looking, I'd've loved you for it. But you sneaked out for the law. That's what a
      cheap dame would do. So tomorrow the Indians can have ya.

(*Marfeu goes to attack Gable behind his back. Joan tosses a frying pan at Marfeu.*)

GABLE: Should I say thanks, baby, or were you just waving at something?
CRAWFORD: Don't thank me. I didn't give you a thing. All I want is to get out of here,
      and you happen to be going my way. So I played you, but the minute I find
      someone going faster than you, I'll. . . .
GABLE: You won't.

FILMOGRAPHY

Dance, Fools, Dance (1931)   *Chained* (1934)
Laughing Sinners (1931)   *Forsaking All Others* (1934)
Possessed (1931)   *Love on the Run* (1936)
Dancing Lady (1933)   *Strange Cargo* (1940)

elegance and class
ASTAIRE & ROGERS

"All the world loves a dancer, don't you?"
Fred Astaire to Ginger Rogers,

SWING TIME (1936)

Katharine Hepburn once said that Ginger Rogers gave Fred Astaire sex appeal, and that he gave her class. Critics have debated this often-quoted comment for years. In fact, the subject is moot because for any successful dance team—and Astaire and Rogers were perhaps the most successful in the history of the movies—it takes two to tango, or to carioca, or to do the continental. "I think when people dance well together, it's because they're sympathetic to each other," Astaire tells Rogers in *The Story of Vernon & Irene Castle*.

How compatible were Astaire and Rogers? By all accounts they were not great friends offscreen, but they both insisted that, in terms of work, they never fought. Pandro Berman, who produced the pair's films for RKO, called their work together "six years of mutual aggression." Whatever their personal feelings, they were nothing short of a miracle on screen.

Astaire danced with many partners during his long career, but, certainly, his most popular alliance was with Rogers. Dance historian John Mueller has eloquently explained the basis for their legendary partnership: "Rogers was outstanding among Astaire's film partners not because she was superior to the others as a dancer, but because, as a skilled, intuitive actress, she was cagey enough to realize that acting did not stop when dancing began. She seemed uniquely to understand the dramatic import of the dance without resorting to style-shattering emoting; she cunningly contributed her

Opposite:
The inimitable Fred Astaire and Ginger Rogers in a studio portrait from *The Barkleys of Broadway*.

share to the choreographic impact of their numbers together. The point of many of these was joy; indeed, the reason so many women have fantasized about dancing with Fred Astaire is that Ginger Rogers conveyed the impression that dancing with him is the most thrilling experience imaginable."

Ah, to dance with Astaire. If Rogers could do it, why not one of us? We could imagine ourselves dancing their dances and singing their songs, for they made it look effortless.

Perhaps dancing seemingly came so easy to Astaire because he had begun so young. He was born Frederick Austerlitz in Omaha, Nebraska, on May 10, 1899. At four, he started ballet lessons with his sister Adele, and within months they were performing in local church halls. Realizing their children possessed an extraordinary gift, the Austerlitzes moved to New York, where Fred and Adele studied dance and worked briefly in vaudeville.

In 1917, they appeared in *Over the Top*, their first show. They had soon achieved stardom and, throughout the 1920s, danced in numerous productions in New York and London. George Gershwin wrote *Lady, Be Good* and *Funny Face* especially for them. Their last show together was *The Band Wagon* in 1931, after which Adele retired to marry Lord Charles Cavendish. "She was a great artist," Astaire said of his sister, "incomparable and inimitable, and the grandest sister anyone could have."

Though the general consensus was that Astaire would never find as good a partner as Adele, a few months later he danced with Claire Luce in the stage production of *The Gay Divorce*. The critics and the public

Astaire and Rogers danced together for the first time in *Flying Down to Rio*. Watching a group of Brazilian dancers
perform a fast tango called "The Carioca," Astaire turns to Rogers and says: "I'd like to try this just once.
Come on." The dance begins with them intimately pressing foreheads in a tight embrace and ends in this extravagant
finale atop a cluster of revolving pianos. Inspired by the famed choreographer, Hermes Pan,
the carioca created a new dance craze in America.

conceded that one Astaire was better than none, and the musical ran for eight months.

According to Hollywood legend, Astaire's first screen test was rejected by a Goldwyn executive, who declared: "Can't act, can't sing, balding, can dance a little." Astaire certainly dispelled the evaluation on all but one count. He was a talented actor both in musicals and, years later, in dramas. (In 1974, he was nominated for the Oscar for best supporting actor for his role in *The Towering Inferno*.) As for his singing, Oscar Levant once commented that Astaire was "the best singer of songs the movie world ever knew." (According to film critic David Shipman, no one except Ethel Merman has ever had more contemporary songs written expressly for him.) Recently, PBS devoted an entire show to Astaire's singing. And volumes have been written about his dancing. As for his hair, granted, Astaire was forced to wear a toupee (which he despised) in most of his films.

Eventually, he signed with RKO, though he made his film debut on loan to MGM, where he played himself, dancing with Joan Crawford in *Dancing Lady*. Then, in 1933, the worst year of the Great Depression, Astaire was assigned the second male lead in *Flying Down to Rio*. The movie was notable for its grand finale, in which a bevy of chorus girls strapped onto the wings of airplanes performed a series of midair acrobatics. Though the number today seems loony to the point of ludicrousness, *Flying Down to Rio* enjoyed a record-breaking three-week run at Radio City Music Hall, grossing more than $18 million and helping rejuvenate a failing RKO. The movie was perhaps more notable, though, for its first-time pairing of Astaire and Rogers.

Born Virginia Katherine McMath, Rogers was raised by her divorced, stage-door mother. In 1925, fourteen-year-old Ginger won out over 120 girls in a Charleston contest; the prize was a four-week vaudeville contract. She married her first husband, Jack Pepper, in 1928, and they formed a dance team, "Ginger and Pepper." When the couple split up, Rogers performed alone until she landed a substantial role on Broadway in *Top Speed*. By 1930, she was earning $1000 a week playing the lead in Gershwin's *Girl Crazy*.

In 1931, Rogers headed for Hollywood, where she was typecast as a dim-witted chorine or wisecracking flapper in several small roles. In *Young Man of Manhattan* she sang: "I got IT, but IT don't do me no good"; in *Gold Diggers of 1933* she sang "We're in the Money" in pig Latin, skimpily dressed in a costume made entirely of coins; and the same year she appeared in *Forty-Second Street* as Anytime Annie ("The only time she ever said no she didn't hear the question."). Then, she was signed by RKO and cast in *Flying Down to Rio*.

Astaire was not happy with this film. He complained that his dancing looked ponderous and that his angular face was all wrong for the big screen. He fled to London, abandoning the idea of ever making another movie. But when the picture was released to rave reviews, the studio cabled Astaire to return home to work with Rogers again.

Astaire was not terribly eager for the assignment. As he wrote his agent, Leland Hayward: "What's all this talk about me being teamed with Ginger Rogers? I will not have it, Leland—I did not get into pictures to be *teamed* with her or anyone else. . . . I don't mind making another picture with her, but as for this team idea, it's out! I've just managed to live down one partnership, and I don't want to be bothered with any more."

In the first romantic duet that Astaire choreographed for Rogers, they dance to Cole Porter's "Night and Day" and show the world that a couple can make love without leaving the dance floor. As if to prove the point, when the number ends, Astaire lowers Rogers onto a bench and offers her a cigarette.

Of course, he relented and returned to Hollywood, where he and Rogers filmed *The Gay Divorcée*. (The Hays Office censors had changed the title from *The Gay Divorce*, insisting that a divorcée could be gay, but not a divorce).

Their second movie did even better than their first, establishing Astaire and Rogers as the premier money-makers on the RKO lot. Between 1933 and 1939, they made nine movies for that studio, each among the most profitable of the hundreds of motion pictures made by RKO during that period. Both in 1935 and the following

the plot. Previously, song-and-dance routines were simply dropped into the plot of a movie; the story stopped for the music and then picked up again once the number ended. In an Astaire-Rogers movie, each dance told a story and illuminated the relationship between the leads. Dance critic Arlene Croce has suggested that Astaire musicals are actually dance films with plots rather than stories with dance.

However they are categorized, though, every Astaire-Rogers film is a love story, even though the stars are always chaste. In several films, he falls madly in love with her at first glance. "I told you I haven't even met her yet," Astaire says in *Shall We Dance?*, "but I'd kind of like to marry her." He makes numerous references to making love to Rogers, in *Top Hat*, saying: "If I ever forgot myself with that girl, I'd remember it." But they didn't share a close-up screen kiss until their ninth (and next-to-last) film together, *The Story of Vernon & Irene Castle*, in 1939.

Actually, they didn't need to kiss in order to show emotion or even sexual attraction. Why kiss her when he could, quite literally, sweep her off her feet? All their sexual energy was channeled into their dancing. When dancing, he was charming, willful, passionate, shy, domineering, and tender. In almost every film, Rogers is never really interested in Astaire until they begin to dance. She may start the number arrogant and unresponsive, but within a few bars she's keeping pace with him, and by the sweeping finale she's melted into his arms.

Many writers have tried to describe Astaire's dancing. *Life* once wrote: "Astaire dances to American rhythms with an air of gay spontaneity that consummately reflects the folk origins of his art. Debonair, exultant, amused, he has imparted to the tap dance an elegance and mobility of which the cloggers and minstrels of the last century never dreamed." In 1936 *Theater Arts* called Astaire's dancing "as modern as the streamlined flier, and as sensitive as the rhythms of the old psalmists." And in his song "You're the Top" Cole Porter extolled "the nimble tread of the feet of Fred Astaire."

To understand the genius of Astaire and his extraordinary contribution to movie musicals, it's crucial to understand how he revolutionized the filming of dance routines. Astaire was not only a choreographer but a designer of camera angles. Before he arrived in Hollywood,

Opposite, clockwise from top left:
The unsurpassed Astaire and Rogers in *Top Hat*, floating in a gondola across Hollywood's Art Deco version of the Lido in Venice; dancing a reprise of the Castle Walk in *The Story of Vernon & Irene Castle*; affirmatively answering the question posed in the title song of the movie, *Shall We Dance?*; and, in *Roberta*, proving that when "Smoke Gets in Your Eyes," it doesn't affect your feet.
Above:
In *Follow the Fleet*, Astaire and Rogers mimic a couple of downcast swells on the verge of suicide, who ultimately come to the conclusion: "Let's Face the Music and Dance."

year, two of their films were top-ten earners, an achievement unsurpassed and only very rarely equalled in the history of Hollywood.

The popularity of these films was due, in part, to the fact that Astaire-Rogers movies virtually redefined the film musical by using music and dance to advance

In *Carefree*, Astaire is a psychiatrist who hypnotizes radio singer Rogers out of her crush on him and into the arms of Ralph Bellamy. Then Astaire realizes he loves her. She once again falls under his spell when he mesmerizes her (and us) in the "Change Partners" number. The dance showcases Rogers's astonishingly fluid body movements, especially her back bends.

dance routines in movies had been shot in pieces. During a sequence, the camera would shift to different parts of the body, for instance, focusing on the feet, moving to the arms, and then pulling back for a long shot of the crowd. Trick shots (the trademark of Busby Berkeley routines) were made by shooting up from the floor, down from the ceiling, or through a gauzy curtain or some latticework.

Reversing this process, Astaire kept the flow of the dance intact. His dance routines were shot with his entire body in full view for the whole number. Three cameras were used for each take, and the best shots of the sequence were pieced together. Filming an average Astaire dance routine took between six and ten complete takes. "He was technically the greatest revolutionary in the history of the movie musical," writes

Arlene Croce. "He forced camerawork, cutting, synchronization and scoring to ever higher standards of sensitivity and precision. He fought on every front, and in the cutting room he was a terror. . . . And no one until that time had insisted on so exact a synchronization of picture and sound."

Astaire worked out his routines with RKO dance director Hermes Pan, who taught them to Rogers. Then the pair would rehearse together, adding new ideas along the way.

Mark Sandrich, director of five Astaire-Rogers musicals, credited Rogers for her contributions to the dances: "You would be surprised how much (Rogers) adds to the numbers. Fred arranges them, and then when they get to rehearsing, Ginger puts in her own suggestions. And they're sensible ones. Fred discusses every one with her at length, and a good many of them are used."

Astaire believed in extensive rehearsals, saying that they allowed for spontaneity: "I think it's probably the secret of the success of the numbers that you know it so well you never have to think about what the next step is. . . . It looks like it just happens. . . . It only comes from rehearsing. It just becomes part of you." A legendary perfectionist, he demanded the best from others, and wasn't satisfied until he delivered it himself. Hermes Pan recalled working with Astaire in a scene from *Carefree* which required him to dance over tables and chairs, up and down halls, and out onto a terrace and a golf course. In rhythm to the music piped in over the loudspeakers, Astaire had to keep dancing and hit a dozen or so golf balls, one after another, on cue and in time with the music. When the crew went to retrieve the balls, they found all of them lying within eight feet of each other.

Astaire supervised every aspect of his films. In the "Cheek to Cheek" number in *Top Hat*, for example, Rogers's ice blue satin dress, which was completely covered in ostrich feathers, caused a major dispute. As the couple began to dance, feathers flew everywhere, blinding Astaire and making him sneeze. He was livid with anger, and she burst into tears. The dress designer spent the entire evening sewing each feather in place, and the next day, though a few feathers still flew, they managed to shoot the scene. From then on, Astaire insisted on checking out his partner's wardrobe before every scene.

Though Astaire and Rogers made their dancing look effortless, it was anything but, as she once explained: "Just try and keep up with those feet sometime! Try and look graceful while thinking where your right hand should be, and how your head should be held, and which foot you end the next eight bars on, and whether you're near enough to the steps to leap up six of them backward without looking. Not to mention those Astaire rhythms. Did you ever count the different tempos he can think up in three minutes?" The work was excruciating. They filmed forty-seven takes of the finale to "Never Gonna Dance" in *Swing Time*; quitting only because Rogers's feet were bleeding so badly they were staining her pale satin slippers.

None of this colossal struggle showed on screen, of course. All the audience ever saw was the final result: elegance and class. As David Shipman writes: "What made the films so popular with contemporary audiences was their gaiety: the ease and imagination of the

Perhaps the song title to this "Never Gonna Dance" number from *Swing Time* should have been renamed: "Never Gonna Dance Any Better Than This."

Ten years after ending their partnership, Astaire and Rogers made *The Barkleys of Broadway*. Though their dancing was still top-drawer, the movie lacked some of the spontaneity of their earlier work. Still, the movie worked because, unlike many other dance teams, both Astaire and Rogers were excellent actors who gave credible performances even when they weren't dancing. Certainly, *The Barkleys of Broadway* remains a fitting tribute to their enduring screen partnership.

. . . dance routines (it has been suggested that the cinema screen was invented expressly for Astaire to gambol on it). . . . Their artistry was considerable, and so were their songs. None of this has dated."

By 1936, though the team was still a top draw, their popularity was showing signs of waning. Also, Astaire was more worried than ever about being associated so closely with one partner. "Pandro Berman has said that he had repeatedly to force the two of them together," writes Arlene Croce. "Personal enmity was not the reason, professional pride was. The same pride that kept them locked together in a cycle of hits, their teamwork getting better and better, made each of them eager to succeed without the other. There was something comic in their predicament: Astaire had forged for himself a new romantic style in the movies, a style that had made people forget he was Adele's brother, and in the forging of it had created a new menace to his own survival. Would they forget he was Ginger Rogers' partner?"

Rogers was eager to explore other projects, especially as a dramatic actress. But before they split for good, they were paired for *Carefree* in 1938 and *The Story of Vernon & Irene Castle* in 1939. In all, they made a total of nine films for RKO, and their success rescued the studio from certain bankruptcy.

Rogers went on to dramatic roles in pictures such as *Kitty Foyle*, for which she won a Best Actress Oscar. By 1945, she was the most highly paid actor in Hollywood, but shortly after that her career went into a decline.

In *Swing Time* Astaire tells Rogers: "I've danced with you, I'm never going to dance again." Fortunately, this was far from the truth. Though he never made as many movies with anyone else, over the course of his long career he danced with Joan Fontaine, Eleanor Powell, Paulette Goddard, Rita Hayworth, Lucille Bremer, Jane Powell, Vera-Ellen, Judy Garland, Leslie Caron, Cyd Charisse, and Audrey Hepburn, among others.

In 1946, he announced his retirement and was released from his MGM contract on the condition that, if he ever decided to return to making movies, he would fulfill his commitment to them. Two years later MGM begged him to replace Gene Kelly, who had broken his ankle while rehearsing *Easter Parade*. Astaire jumped at the chance and, along with Judy Garland, turned the Irving Berlin musical into a major box-office hit. The two were signed to star again in *The Barkleys of Broadway*, but Garland fell ill and was replaced by Rogers.

It had been ten years since Astaire and Rogers's last film together, and the reunion was quite successful, helping also to revive Rogers's career. In the 1950s she appeared in more mature movie roles. She had a comeback on Broadway in the late 1960s, replacing Carol Channing in *Hello Dolly!*, and, a few years later, starring in the London production of *Mame*.

After *The Barkleys of Broadway*, Astaire abandoned any idea of retiring. He went on to star in many more musicals, including *The Band Wagon* with Cyd Charisse and *Funny Face* with Audrey Hepburn. When musicals went out of fashion in the late 1950s, Astaire took supporting roles in such dramas as *On the Beach* and *The Towering Inferno*. He appeared on TV and hosted the 1976 film, *That's Entertainment Part Two*. He died in 1987, at the age of eighty-eight.

From the moment of his first appearance on screen, Astaire assumed the status of a Hollywood legend, and his films with Rogers attest to his genius. As John Mueller has observed: "Over the course of his long film career, Fred Astaire appeared in 212 musical numbers, of which 133 contain fully developed dance routines. At least seventy-five of these dance numbers seem to me to be at or near the masterpiece level, and there is a great deal of highly impressive choreography and dancing among the less masterful dances as well. There are some clinkers, but these are remarkably few in number, and most were choreographed by others. In quantity, and especially in quality, Astaire's contribution is unrivaled in films, and indeed, has few parallels in the history of dance."

In the 1930s, Gene Kelly said that "fifty years from now, the only one of today's dancers who will be remembered is Fred Astaire." It was, perhaps, the perfect rebuttal to Astaire's observation at the opening of *Swing Time:* "Hoofing is all right, but there's no future in it."

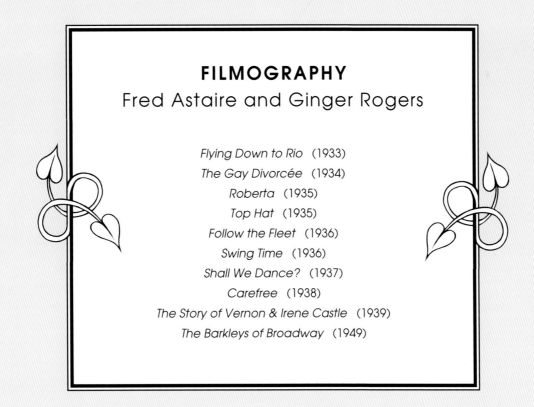

FILMOGRAPHY
Fred Astaire and Ginger Rogers

Flying Down to Rio (1933)

The Gay Divorcée (1934)

Roberta (1935)

Top Hat (1935)

Follow the Fleet (1936)

Swing Time (1936)

Shall We Dance? (1937)

Carefree (1938)

The Story of Vernon & Irene Castle (1939)

The Barkleys of Broadway (1949)

Several frames from the marvelous "Isn't This a Lovely Day" routine in *Top Hat.* Rogers wears the infamous flying-feathers gown that drove Astaire to distraction, but, aside from that, isn't this a lovely dance?

He talks; she pouts.
He breaks into song; she listens, sort of.
He dances; she reluctantly joins him.
Before too long, she is his, body and soul.

Fred Astaire and Ginger Rogers

All Astaire-Rogers love scenes are played out in
    movement to music.
Why should they talk when they could dance?
And, oh, how they danced!

sophistication LOY & POWELL

LOY: It's a dirty trick to bring me all the way to
          New York just to make a widow out of me.
POWELL: You wouldn't be a widow long.
LOY: You bet I wouldn't!
POWELL: Not with all your money.

THE THIN MAN (1934)

In *The Great Ziegfeld*, William Powell plays the flamboyant producer Florenz Ziegfeld, and Myrna Loy appears as Billie Burke, Ziegfeld's second wife and a star of stage and screen.

In a prophetic scene Powell proposes to Loy, saying: "I haven't anything to offer you because there's nothing you really seem to need. You've made the most of yourself unassisted, and that's grand. You're a great star already, so there's little I can offer you. Nothing I can give you except my love." A knowing Loy replies: "That isn't enough. I'd expect part of your ambition, half of your trouble, two-thirds of your worries, and all of your respect."

Now, there was a proposal worthy of the most popular married couple in movie history. From 1934 to 1947, they costarred in fourteen movies, working together more often than either Astaire and Rogers or Tracy and Hepburn. In every one of their films Loy and Powell were married either when the movie started or by the last reel. And they were always equal partners, whether as Billie Burke and Florenz Ziegfeld or as the infamous Nick and Nora Charles.

Opposite:
In *Libeled Lady* Powell tricks Loy into falling for him
and then finds himself in love with her.
Right:
Loy and Powell always played the quintessential happily
married couple. In *The Great Ziegfeld* she is Billie Burke, his
second wife. As the photos show, they age gracefully together
in the film, which they also certainly did throughout
their long career together.

Manhattan Melodrama was the first movie starring Loy and Powell. At the start of the film Loy is in love with Clark Gable but not his gangster lifestyle, so she leaves him to marry Powell. It was during the filming of this movie that director Woody Van Dyke noted the rapport between Loy and Powell and decided to cast them as Nick and Nora Charles in *The Thin Man*.

Ironically, both Powell and Loy began their careers being typecast in roles much different than those of the sophisticated Charleses. Loy was born in Helena, Montana, in 1905 and moved to Los Angeles in 1919, where she began her career as a dancer. She was signed by Warner and appeared in a number of silent movies playing exotic women, usually of mixed Oriental origin. In *Thirteen Women* (1932) she plays a Javanese-Indian half-caste, who murders all of the white school-mates who patronized her. The character couldn't have been farther from the real Loy. "Wouldn't you know," director John Ford once complained, "the kid they pick to play tramps is the only good girl in Hollywood."

Producer Irving Thalberg brought Loy to MGM in the early '30s. She was one of the few actresses to successfully make the transition from silent films to talkies, even though in many of her early talking pictures she was forced to speak Pidgin English. She had a face that the camera adored, yet, unlike the unapproachable Garbo, Loy's beauty was accessible. Charles Laughton

As a married couple in *Manhattan Melodrama*, Loy and Powell project great warmth and sexuality. Though their kissing scenes are tame by today's standards, the couple convinces us that they are actually in love.

Two swells out on the town in *Manhattan Melodrama*. She's drenched in fur, and
he's wrapped in silk scarves, even when they're dining on deli and beer. Still, they were the epitome of sophistication,
and they seemed to really like each other. Powell claimed they weren't really acting; they were
in perfect harmony as both actors and friends.

once aptly described her as "Venus de Milo at the inter-section of Hollywood and Vine."

William Powell's looks were equally accessible. He was born in Pittsburgh in 1892 and made his Broadway debut in 1912. After becoming a successful stage actor, he began his career in silent movies, playing the kind of sleazy villain audiences love to hate. He was first paired with Loy in 1934 for *Manhattan Melodrama*, which also costarred Clark Gable. In this film about two orphans who grow up together on the streets of New York and take different paths in life, Gable turns gangster and Powell becomes an honest politician. Loy, the love interest for both men, winds up married to Powell. Today, the plot seems clichéd, but it was the first of its

kind, and Arthur Caesar won an Oscar for the screenplay. The movie was a box-office hit, garnering publicity when real-life gangster John Dillinger came out of hiding to see the movie and was gunned down by FBI agents in front of the Biograph Theater in Chicago.

Loy met Powell on the set of *Manhattan Melodrama,* and in her autobiography she describes the encounter: "My first scene with Bill, a night shot on the back lot, happened before we'd even met. Woody (W. S. Van Dyke, the director of the film) was apparently too busy for introductions. My instructions were to run out of a building, through a crowd, and into a strange car. When Woody called 'Action,' I opened the car door, jumped in and landed smack in William Powell's lap. He looked up nonchalantly: 'Miss Loy, I presume?' I said: 'Mr. Powell?' And that's how I met the man who would be my partner in fourteen films."

In *Manhattan Melodrama* Loy and Powell banter in a way that would become typical of their characters in future films. "I'm not complaining," says Loy. "I'm just wasting the best years of my life waiting in a taxi." In telling Loy his life story Powell says: "I was born at home because I wanted to be near my mother at the time."

W. S. Van Dyke noted the chemistry between Loy and Powell on the set; they joked a lot and seemed to have an instant rapport, matching wits with an easy style and grace. Van Dyke suggested the team for *The Thin Man.*

He had bought the screen rights to Dashiell Hammett's novel mainly because he was fascinated by the relationship between Nick and Nora Charles. Van Dyke was a happily married man, and he felt movies unfairly emphasized the negative aspects of long-term relationships, stressing jealousy, infidelity, and deceit over compatibility and love. He wanted to make a film in which a married couple actually enjoyed being with each other.

Louis B. Mayer agreed to cast Powell as the detective, mostly on the strength of Powell's previous work as the lead in several Philo Vance movies. But Mayer objected to Loy as Nora. After all, the public still knew her as an exotic vamp. Van Dyke not only insisted on

Left:
**Myrna Loy and William Powell were perfectly cast
as Nick and Nora Charles,
able to solve murders with a gun,
a wise crack, and a martini shaker.**

While Nick was in charge of solving the crime, Nora was never far behind him, either eavesdropping or edging her way into the heart of the mystery. "I think you better let us go alone," Nick tells her in *The Thin Man.* "Catch me trying to let you go alone," she replies.

Loy, but threatened to walk out if he couldn't get her. Mayer finally relented, but only under the condition that the filming be completed in three weeks so Loy would be free for her next movie.

Once the team was hired, Van Dyke ordered the script rewritten to add at least six romantic scenes between the leads. The new dialogue highlighted their rapport. "You got types?" Nora asks Nick. "Only you darling, lanky brunettes with wicked jaws," he replies. By some miracle, *The Thin Man* was completed on schedule, and it opened in 1934. (Known at MGM as "One-Take Woody," Van Dyke actually shot the entire movie in sixteen days!)

The Thin Man not only made major stars of Myrna Loy and William Powell but also catapulted Asta, the dog, to fame and fortune. In *After the Thin Man* Asta becomes crucial to the plot when he swallows a key piece of evidence. "Look at him running around with a clue in him," remarks the ever cool-headed Loy.

No one at MGM had any idea that *The Thin Man* would become a hit, much less spawn five sequels. In fact, MGM executives worried about the picture. Sam Marx, the head of the story department at the time, explained: "The whole thing broke with tradition in several ways. . . . The matrimonial combination of Powell and Loy . . . was a risk because in those days you got married at the end of the movie, not at the beginning. Marriage wasn't supposed to be fun. . . . (The) first preview was a thermometer that told us how much heat the team was generating. They had a chemistry that came out of Myrna Loy and William Powell, plus the characters of Nick and Nora Charles."

Indeed, audiences in the mid 1930s loved the Charleses. "It was 1934—a grim Depression year," writes

Powell's biographer, Charles Francisco, "and real husbands and wives found joy in being able to identify with such a wacky, wonderful couple who had no money worries."

Loy felt the success of *The Thin Man* was due to the crackling sexuality she and Powell had generated. "What made *The Thin Man* series work, what made it fun, was that we didn't attempt to hide the fact that sex is part of marriage," she writes. "But it was deft, done with delicacy and humor. Then, too, the Charleses had enormous tolerance for each other's imperfections. . . . *The Thin Man* virtually introduced modern marriage to the screen."

True enough, but Loy and Powell themselves projected magic as a couple. In 1983, noted director George Cukor explained the enormous appeal of the team: "There had been romantic couples before, but Loy and Powell were something new and original. They actually made marital comedy palatable. I remember Bill Powell when he started out as a melodramatic actor. Then, by some alchemy, he suddenly became comic. But Myrna gave the wit to the whole thing. They hit that wonderful note because he always did a wee bit too much and she underdid it, creating a grace, a charm, a chemistry."

Whatever the reasons for its success, *The Thin Man* represented a turning point in the careers of both stars. Powell's career had desperately needed a boost. By 1933, he was considered a washed-up actor. He had been released from his contract with Warner Brothers, and MGM hesitantly offered him a one-picture deal on *Manhattan Melodrama.* The success of that film, combined with the unexpected triumph of *The Thin Man,*dispelled any doubts about Powell, and MGM gave him a long-term contract.

The Thin Man also made Loy a major star, even though she had already appeared in more than seventy films. After 1934 Loy was cast over and over as the perfect wife. She didn't exactly love the characterization, saying she preferred Gore Vidal's description of her as "the eternal good-sex woman-wife." This casting was in some ways ironic because Loy could never find in her personal life what came so easily to her on screen. She married four times, and she never had any children.

Offscreen, Loy and Powell were often mistaken for a married couple. "We became close friends, but contrary to popular belief, we were never *really* married or even close to it," writes Loy. "Oh, there were times when Bill had a crush on me and times when I had a crush on Bill, but we never made anything of it. We worked around it and stayed pals."

Powell once said: "My friends never fail to tell me that the smartest thing I ever did was marry Myrna Loy on the screen. And it was the pleasantest (experience), I might add. . . . When we did a scene together, we forgot about technique, camera angles, and microphones. We weren't acting. We were just two people in perfect harmony."

To cash in on the popularity of Loy and Powell, MGM starred them in *Evelyn Prentice* and *After the Thin Man*, which didn't quite achieve the critical praise of its prequel but was a box-office smash nonetheless. Both films built on Nick's reputation as a drinker. In *The Thin Man* a re-

Powell is a trial lawyer in *Evelyn Prentice* who must cross-examine his wife, Loy, for the murder of a playboy with whom she might have had an affair. What is most implausible about this movie is the idea of infidelity between Loy and Powell.

porter inquires: "Is he working on any cases?" and Nora says: "Yes, a case of scotch." In *After the Thin Man* Nora asks: "Darling, are you packing?" and, gulping a martini, Nick replies: "Just putting away the liquor."

Nick's disdain for respectability is another running theme in the series. When Nick asks Nora about a certain couple she says: "You wouldn't know them, darling, they're respectable." Later, Nick tells the chauffeur: "We want to go someplace and get the taste of respectability out of our mouths."

Nick's low-life friends appear in all the sequels spouting such lines as: "What do you mean illiterate? My mother and father were married at City Hall." Or: "Well, cut off my legs and call me Shorty." And the camera immediately cuts to Nora's reaction. Nick might be suave, but Nora is the epitome of cool; nothing ruffles her designer feathers. She plays poker in the baggage car of a train or calmly reacts to an assortment of hoods and scoundrels soaking the Charleses for their last bottle of scotch. She's equal to Nick in every way, and in love with him as well. A wonderful listener, she's totally absorbed in whatever he says. She never doubts her man. She's smart and she's brave. Several of the films end with Nora throwing herself in front of a gun to save Nick.

Most of the *Thin Man* sequels featured paper-thin plots. Full of red herrings and convoluted twists, the stories often got too confusing to follow. But who cared? The films worked because of the relationship between Nick and Nora.

In 1936, Loy and Powell went to San Francisco to shoot exteriors for *After the Thin Man*. They were joined by Jean Harlow, whom Powell had met in 1934, around the time the Charleses had first appeared. "I realized during that trip how deeply she (Harlow) loved Bill, a total, childlike love, full of the exuberance and wonder that characterized her," Loy writes. A year later, while Loy and Powell were shooting the slapstick comedy *Double Wedding*, Harlow died. It was a crushing blow to Powell, who collapsed during the filming. Production was delayed several times, and the strain of his ordeal showed in the film. Loy felt that Powell "blamed himself for Jean's death: he had loved her but hadn't married her and taken her away from her mother."

A life-threatening bout with cancer exacerbated this traumatic time for Powell. In 1939, he returned to MGM to work on *Another Thin Man*. In January 1940,

This page:

Double Wedding pits Powell and Loy against one another as two antagonists who hate each other until they realize it's really love. While Powell was making this film, his then-fiance, Jean Harlow, suddenly died.

Opposite (clockwise from top left):

Another Thin Man introduces baby Nick Charles, Jr. "What's the idea of the kid?" asks one of Nick's associates. "Well, we had a dog and he was lonesome," cracks Powell.

In *I Love You Again* Powell suffers amnesia and astonishes Loy with his new personality.

Finally, in two scenes from *Love Crazy* Powell pretends to be insane in order to win back Loy's love.

Powell met and married starlet Diana Lewis, who was twenty-six years his junior. The couple had known each other for only three weeks when they were married. Hollywood gossips gave the union a year, at most, but the marriage lasted forty years.

Loy and Powell continued to work together. *I Love You Again* was their ninth movie in six years, and the title was a private joke to the stars, who said they'd never be allowed to love anyone else on screen. And in *Love Crazy,* they played a long-married couple still in love with each other.

In 1947, Loy was disputing her contract with MGM just as they were about to begin shooting *Song of the Thin Man,* the fifth entry in the series. MGM was anxious to keep the sequels coming and, according to Powell, "announced new Noras, like Irene Dunne, from time to time—merely as a ploy, I suspect, to lure Myrna back—but every time such sacrilege appeared in the columns, there was an uproar. The studio was deluged with fan letters. The fans wanted Myrna, and they didn't want anyone else. I wanted Myrna, too."

Loy and Powell appeared together for the very last time in *The Senator Was Indiscreet* (1947), in which she has only a cameo at the finale. Throughout the film Powell, an inept senator, telephones "Momma," his wife, whenever he has a problem. At the end of the film he winds up on a tropical island with the mysterious Momma, Myrna Loy in a sarong. This was the only film ever directed by playwright George S. Kaufman, and Loy did it as a favor to him. The studio, Universal, paid her with a Cadillac, as they couldn't afford her usual fee.

Leaving MGM after thirteen years, Loy successfully continued her acting career, often playing the perfect wife in such notable pictures as *The Best Years of Our Lives* and *Mr. Blandings Builds His Dream House.* Also an activist in political affairs, working for the United Nations, she campaigned for various Democrats and spoke out for causes that were dear to her heart. She enjoyed a successful stage career later in her life.

Opposite:
Loy and Powell continued to crank out more *Thin Man* films, such as *Song of the Thin Man* (top) and *Shadow of the Thin Man* (bottom). As the series progressed the plots got weaker, but the relationship between Nick and Nora was so much fun to watch that the series was wildly successful at the box office.
Right:
Powell, Loy, and Asta in *The Thin Man Goes Home*.

In 1956, Universal tried to lure Loy and Powell into making a television film, casting them yet again as a married couple. Loy was eager to do the project after a nine-year hiatus from their partnership. When she arrived in Hollywood, she received dozens of red roses from Powell,.along with the news that he'd decided not to do the movie. He retired from films at the age of sixty-five, and she did the film with Melvyn Douglas instead.

William Powell died in 1984, at the age of ninety-one. For weeks after his death, Loy received condolences from friends, as if she'd lost a husband. "Well, our screen partnership lasted through fourteen pictures, longer than any of my marriages," writes Loy. "To this day, forty years after our last appearance together, people consider us a couple."

It's hard to calculate the influence of Loy and Powell. Certainly, they created a prototype for romantic comedy on film. Producer Ross Hunter, for example, says: "Myrna was my heroine. She was the clone for the stars I used, chic even in dungarees. I owe my big-gest breakthrough as a producer to her. I studied her comedies with William Powell. I ran eight of their pictures and got the idea of doing *Pillow Talk* (in 1959). I modeled my stars on Powell and Loy: took Doris Day out of the kitchen; put Rock Hudson in tails. People said that romantic comedy came of age with *Pillow Talk*. Well, if that's true, I can't take all the credit. It was Powell and Loy."

Offscreen, Loy and Powell have influenced generations of movie lovers. In 1984 humorist Cynthia Heimel wrote: "Whenever I'm too crazy, too paranoiac, or too mentally feeble to deal with a situation, I pretend I'm Myrna Loy. It works. . . . (*Note:* If you're a man, it might be more profitable to pretend you're William Powell as Nicky, another perfect role model.)" More than fifty years after they first appeared together on screen, Powell and Loy continue to set the standard for sophisticated behavior. And, in 1991, Loy was recognized by her peers when she received a special Honorary Oscar for a lifetime of achievement in films.

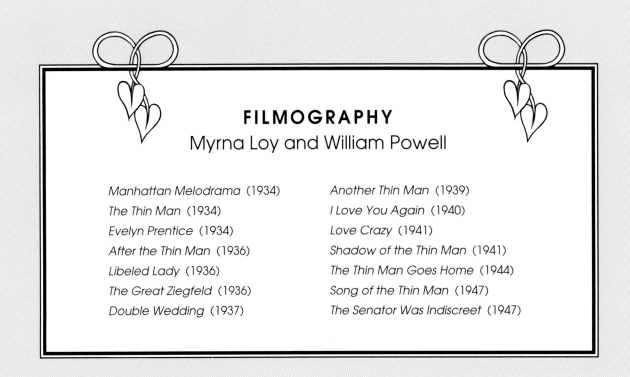

FILMOGRAPHY
Myrna Loy and William Powell

Manhattan Melodrama (1934)

The Thin Man (1934)

Evelyn Prentice (1934)

After the Thin Man (1936)

Libeled Lady (1936)

The Great Ziegfeld (1936)

Double Wedding (1937)

Another Thin Man (1939)

I Love You Again (1940)

Love Crazy (1941)

Shadow of the Thin Man (1941)

The Thin Man Goes Home (1944)

Song of the Thin Man (1947)

The Senator Was Indiscreet (1947)

TYPICAL LOVE SCENE

Myrna Loy & William Powell

Many of their scenes consist of a few crackling one-liners, the rattle of a cocktail shaker, and a quick kiss, usually on the run. Sophisticated quips and rapid rejoinders best typify their relationship. Here's a sampling:

POWELL: Darling, you aon't need mystery, you have something more alluring.
LOY: What?
POWELL: Me.

AFTER THE THIN MAN

* * *

LOY: We had a lovely trip; Nick was sober in Kansas City.

ANOTHER THIN MAN

* * *

POWELL: I thought that was rather clever of me.
LOY: Yes, I thought you thought so.

LIBELED LADY

* * *

POWELL: Make any New Year's resolutions?
LOY: Not yet. Any complaints or suggestions?
POWELL: Few.
LOY: Which?
POWELL: Complaints.
LOY: All right, shoot.
POWELL: Well, you don't scold, you don't nag, and you look far too pretty in the mornings.
LOY: All right, I'll remember: must scold, must nag, mustn't be too pretty in the morning.

AFTER THE THIN MAN

POWELL: If this rampage of respectability persists, we'll have to get you a bulletproof girdle.

AFTER THE THIN MAN

* * *

POWELL: Let's get something to eat. I'm thirsty.

AFTER THE THIN MAN

* * *

POWELL: I'd hate to wake up one morning and find the fortune I married you for was gone. Of course, I could always earn a living as a detective, but what worries me is, what are you and Nicky going to live on?

ANOTHER THIN MAN

* * *

LOY: I got rid of all those reporters.
POWELL: What did you tell them?
LOY: We're out of scotch.
POWELL: What a gruesome idea.

ANOTHER THIN MAN

* * *

LOY: He's more like his father every day.
MAID: He sure is. This morning he was playing with a corkscrew.

SHADOW OF THE THIN MAN

sentimental love
MACDONALD & EDDY

"Your dream prince, reporting for duty!"
Nelson Eddy to Jeanette MacDonald

ROSE MARIE (1936)

About midway through Woody Allen's *Bananas*, the dictator of San Marcos orders his henchmen to torture one of the rebel soldiers of the fictional island. "We keep playing to him the entire score from *Naughty Marietta*," the henchman reports. "It will make him talk." And indeed it does. Over the refrain of "Tramp, Tramp, Tramp" the besieged prisoner begs: "Oh, please, no more. I can't stand operetta. Please, I'll talk, I'll talk, but please cut it off. *Please!*"

Naughty Marietta, the first film to team Jeanette MacDonald and Nelson Eddy, might qualify as torture to some. "High camp" might be a kinder description, but in its day the film (and its stars) were enormously popular at the box office. *Maytime,* the couple's third outing, was the highest grossing film of 1937, when *Screen World* named them the "King and Queen of the Screen." In January of that year, MacDonald and Eddy were voted best female and best male singer in the movies by *Modern Screen.* The rousing finale to *Babes In Arms* features Garland and Rooney tunefully extolling the glories of "God's Country," which include the Rocky Mountains, lots of water, and Nelson Eddy. In their heyday, Jeanette MacDonald and Nelson Eddy were known as "America's Sweethearts" and the "Songbirds of the Depression," and millions of fans flocked to their films.

**MGM often used hand-drawn illustrations
to promote their famous singing sweethearts.
Opposite:
(Clockwise from top left) *The Girl of the Golden West,
Bitter Sweet, I Married an Angel, New Moon.*
Right:
Rose Marie. The poses were always the same,
as were the smiles.**

What made them so popular? Their films were pure escapism, mostly palm court romances featuring elaborate sets, immense costumes, ever-chaste love, and, of course, singing. In any MacDonald-Eddy movie, someone was apt to break into an aria from *Tosca* at the drop of a feathered hat. Perhaps these movies appealed to an immigrant nation, people who'd grown up on vaudeville in the days preceding entry of America into World War II. Apparently, Louis B. Mayer loved these films. For a while at least, Jeanette MacDonald was

Mayer's favorite singer, and she sang "Ah, Sweet Mystery of Life" at his funeral in October 1957.

A singing star of the legitimate theater, MacDonald arrived in Hollywood in 1929 to film *The Love Parade* for famed director Ernst Lubitsch. She was probably twenty-eight years old, though her birth year has been variously given as 1901, 1906, and 1907. She gained a reputation as a comedienne and starred in several light comedies. But Mayer wanted her to do musicals, and, especially for her, MGM bought the Broadway stage musical *I Married an Angel,* which had a score by Rodgers and Hart. However, the project proved too spicy for the Hays code and was shelved.

In 1934, MacDonald appeared in *The Cat and the Fiddle* with Roman Novarro. She had agreed to star in *Naughty Marietta,* but MGM didn't have a leading man, so the project was abandoned for a year. Then, the studio decided to cast tenor Nelson Eddy as MacDonald's costar.

Eddy was well known for his work in concerts and radio when MGM signed him in the early '30s. But the studio didn't give him any work to do. Supposedly, Nelson wasn't all that interested in films, but thought movie publicity would boost his singing career. In any case, he was frustrated by the way MGM ignored him.

Director George Sidney relates how Eddy got his first, minuscule role in films: "A singer named Gene Mallin was coming out of a café when he accidentally put his car in reverse and went off the pier. He had a small role in a film, and rather than wait for him to recover from his injuries, word went out to find somebody who fit his wardrobe. A nobody named Nelson Eddy was just large enough, and they threw him into Gene's clothes."

Eddy's musical debut was in *Broadway to Hollywood* (1933). He then appeared in the finale of the Crawford-Gable hit *Dancing Lady* and sang a Bolero specialty number in *Student Tour* (1934). How he got the lead in *Naughty Marietta* is unclear, though some sources say MacDonald picked Eddy from a batch of photographs.

Left:
MacDonald is a blueblood princess disguised as a scullery maid and Eddy's a mercenary scout ("Here's to men who love to fight!") who saves her from pirates in *Naughty Marietta.* Ultimately, Eddy proves to be a real man who's not afraid to declare his love in public and in song.

Based on an operetta from 1910, *Naughty Marietta* fairly creaks with worn-out dialogue, which ricochets back and forth between "I love you" and "I hate you." MacDonald plays a royal princess who flees France to avoid marrying the noble toady to whom her mean uncle has promised her. Disguised as a scullery maid on a ship headed for Louisiana, she's taken hostage when pirates capture the boat. Fleeing the pirates, she runs right into the arms of Eddy. Although he saves her and her friends and returns them safely to New Orleans, according to Marietta "he's still just a rude, crude colonial."

No matter. He's not interested in her, either. "A petticoat for any length of time is smallpox to the nerves," he says.

Her uncle soon arrives in New Orleans to drag her back to France, and after various misunderstandings MacDonald and Eddy come to realize: "'Tis love, and love alone, the world is seeking. 'Tis love, and love alone, I've waited for. . . ." Even though she's royalty and he's only a lowly colonist, they're meant to be together. As Eddy rhetorically asks: "Do I want to live this foolish life if I can't have you?"

In the end, they escape into pioneer country, singing "Ah! Sweet Mystery of Life." (Eddy later sang this tune at the funeral of Jean Harlow, after MacDonald sang "Indian Love Call." Apparently, they were also the songbirds of Hollywood funerals.)

It was obvious from the very beginning of *Naughty Marietta* that while Eddy could carry a tune, he was no actor. Frightfully stiff in front of the camera, he couldn't remember any of his lines on the first day of shooting. He accidentally walked into a tree (a moment that was kept in the film). Director W. S. Van Dyke became so frustrated on the set that he once shouted: "I've handled Indians, African natives, South Sea Islanders, rhinos, pygmies, and Eskimos and made them act—but not Nelson Eddy."

In spite of everything, the movie was an amazing box-office hit. The *New York Daily News* raved: "MacDonald-Eddy are the new team sensation of the industry." *Naughty Marietta* established them as one of the most successful teams in movie history, and set the pattern for most of their subsequent films.

In their next film, *Rose Marie,* she's a headstrong opera singer roaming the Canadian woods in search of her escaped convict brother, played by a very young Jimmy Stewart. Also looking for Stewart is Canadian Mountie Eddy, who's brave but none too bright. It takes him half the movie to realize that Stewart's character name, Flower, is English for de Flor, MacDonald's name.

Rose Marie features the signature MacDonald-Eddy song "Indian Love Call," which he croons several times. Even after MacDonald leaves the woods to return to the stage, she only has to hum a few bars of the tune for Eddy to appear. This is a frequent happenstance in their movies. Even more often, MacDonald hears Eddy before she actually sees him. In *Maytime* she is so drawn to the sound of his voice she walks into an all-male barroom.

In *Rose Marie*, MacDonald has to tramp through the glorious Canadian wilderness to find the love of her life and be transformed from a glamour girl into a girl scout.

In *Maytime* MacDonald and Eddy literally share "one day to remember for the rest of our lives" and then part for seven years. They're briefly reunited before he dies. Though their love is chaste, she remains faithful.

Eddy was never more unbelievable than when he played a Spanish desperado in *The Girl of the Golden West*, spouting a barely discernable dialect for such lines as "Forever and forever I will love you, Señorita."

That the plots of their films were patently ridiculous didn't seem to matter to their fans. MacDonald-Eddy films are catalogues of sentimentality and romantic devices. He saves her from Spanish desperadoes in *The Girl of the Golden West* and from pirates in *New Moon* and *Naughty Marietta*. Bands of roving gypsies often appear from out of nowhere just so MacDonald and Eddy can join them in song, as in *Maytime* and *Naughty Marietta*. He writes her daily love notes in *Sweethearts*, and she treasures each one. He often serenades her while she stands gazing dreamily from her balcony.

Even death doesn't part these lovers. When Eddy dies in *Bitter Sweet*, MacDonald lives on with his singing ghost. "Carl didn't die. I did, a little," she declares, "And when I sing, I hear him." So do we. He dies again in *Maytime*, and she sings to his ghost. And when she also dies, their ghosts sing to each other until the movie mercifully ends.

In all these movies, their characters have an equality even though one is usually of noble, and the other of lowly, origin. In *Rose Marie*, for example, Eddy proves himself to be brave in the woods, though MacDonald's afraid of animals and noises. "Aren't you afraid of anything?" she asks. Yes, he says, he's afraid of performing on stage, in front of thousands of people, the way she does every night.

In all their movies, love is completely idealized, sanitized, and virginal. There's almost never a hint of sexuality. Eddy and MacDonald rarely even kiss. In *New Moon* he kisses her hand, and then spends several minutes (a movie eternity) begging her forgiveness. In *Maytime* they only kiss once, before he dies, but it's apparently enough to leave her grieving for the rest of her life.

Interestingly, sex between them is hinted at only once, in the last film they made together, *I Married an*

Angel. This was the same property Mayer had commissioned for MacDonald when she was first signed by MGM. It had been rejected for its suggestive plot in 1933, but by the early '40s sentiment had changed.

Here, MacDonald, an angel, comes down from heaven to marry playboy Eddy. They spend the night together (which we know because she wakes up in his bed in the morning). Audiences at the time were shocked. Even Eddy had had misgivings, as he told an interviewer: "In our films together, Miss MacDonald and I always depicted pure love, and we had a lot of trouble with this script because religious groups disapproved of an angel going to bed with a man. Everybody on the lot told us it was either going to be the best picture we ever did or the worst. It was the worst. It took the studio years to figure out how to present it without offending anybody, and then they slashed it to pieces. When we finished it, it was a horrible mess."

Critics agreed. "At best Jeanette MacDonald and Nelson Eddy are not exactly a pair of sylphs, and no one should willfully embarrass them by asking that they pretend that they are," wrote Bosley Crowther in the *New York Times.*

Not only did *I Married an Angel* flop, but it effectively ended the film career of MacDonald and Eddy as a screen couple. Actually, by 1942 their costly films were showing diminishing returns, and after the failure of *I Married an Angel* Eddy was released from his contract.

His film career never recovered. He landed a few minor roles in four films, did concerts and records, and then hit the nightclub circuit, singing songs from musical shows. Eddy was reunited with MacDonald for a few radio broadcasts rehashing their past film successes. In 1964, producer Ross Hunter offered them parts in his Doris Day movie, *The Thrill of It All,* but they declined. In

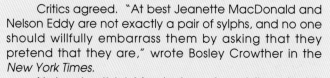

Sage remarks:
Left:
"Forever we'll be sweethearts," Eddy croons
to MacDonald in *Sweethearts.*
Above:
In *New Moon* he declares, "the moon is new but love is old."
True, they don't make movies like they used to.
Thank goodness.

1967, at age sixty-six Eddy died of a heart attack while appearing on stage in Australia.

MacDonald, who had always been more popular, fared slightly better, but when her contract expired in 1942, MGM also let her go. She performed grand opera for a while, returned briefly to play a mother in two minor MGM films, and then went into semiretirement. From time to time, she appeared in cabaret acts and summer stock.

MacDonald was happily married for twenty-eight years to actor Gene Raymond, who had starred with Harlow and Gable in *Red Dust*. The couple had no children. She died of heart failure in 1965, her age variously reported between fifty-eight and sixty-four.

After her death, Allen York wrote in the *Chicago Tribune*: "The passing of Jeanette MacDonald makes us realize that the era of gay, lighthearted and romantic operetta on the silver screen is ended. Nelson Eddy and Jeanette MacDonald—there was a team! Her fragile beauty, dainty manner and magnificent voice were a heritage never to be forgotten, a heritage that abounds with the best melodic traditions of the movies."

MGM had some success with a revival of their films in the 1950s. Many are now available on videocassette. Fans of MacDonald and Eddy remain remarkably faithful; an International Jeanette MacDonald Fan Club still exists.

Left top:
"The bitter with the sweet. That's Vienna,"
and that's the setting for *Bitter Sweet*. MacDonald and Eddy
are starving artists teaching students in exchange for chickens;
though, somehow, through the magic of Hollywood,
they dress remarkably well.
Left bottom:
Eddy is the most eligible bachelor in Budapest and,
for once, he's royalty in *I Married an Angel*, while MacDonald
is a lowly bank clerk. She arrives at his costume party dressed
like an angel and then proves she really is one. If any movie
could end a long and profitable screen partnership,
this was the one to do it.

TYPICAL LOVE SCENE
Jeanette MacDonald and Nelson Eddy

In all their films, MacDonald and Eddy communicate through song.
Their love scenes are also accompanied by a full orchestra,
even when the action takes place in the Canadian wilderness.
"Indian Love Call" is certainly one of their signature numbers.
Written by Otto Harbach, Rudolf Friml, and Oscar Hammerstein II,
the lyrics perfectly symbolize the kind of sentiment offered
in almost every one of their movies.

"INDIAN LOVE CALL"

"Ohh!
Ohh!
So echoes of sweet love notes gently fall
Thru the forest stillness, as fond waiting Indian
    lovers call!
When the lone lagoon
Stirs in the spring,
Welcoming home some swanny white wing,
When the maiden moon,
Riding the sky, gathers her star-eyed dream child
    nigh:
That is the time of the moon and the year,

When love dreams to Indian maidens appear.
And this is the song that they hear:
When I'm calling you—oo-oo-oo—oo-oo-oo!
Will you answer too—oo-oo-oo—oo-oo-oo?
That means I offer my love to you to be your
    own.
If you refuse me, I will be blue.
And waiting all alone,
But if when you hear my love call ringing clear,
And I hear you answering each echo so dear,
Then I will know our love will come true,
You'll belong to me, I'll belong to you!"

FILMOGRAPHY

Naughty Marietta (1935)
Rose Marie (1936)
Maytime (1937)
The Girl of the Golden West (1938)

Sweethearts (1938)
New Moon (1940)
Bitter Sweet (1940)
I Married an Angel (1942)

adventure
FLYNN & DE HAVILLAND

"It's the world against us and us against the world."
Errol Flynn, CAPTAIN BLOOD (1935)

"He's chivalrous to the point of idiocy."
Olivia de Havilland, CAPTAIN BLOOD (1935)

Errol Flynn and Olivia de Havilland were teamed to-gether for the first time in *Captain Blood*, a remake of a popular silent film based on a novel by Rafael Sabatini. Ironically, both actors won their parts by default. The original leads were Bette Davis and Robert Donat. When Donat suffered an attack of appendicitis, George Brent was tested for the role, but he looked too effeminate in the long-haired wigs, so Flynn, who had been cast in another role in the film, was given the lead. Davis had scheduling problems, so the studio tested Jean Muir, Anita Louise, and Joan Bennett. Finally, they decided to hire an unknown actress, nineteen-year-old Olivia de Havilland, who had only appeared in a few minor roles. The casting of two relative unknowns was a risky decision, as *Captain Blood* was a major produc-tion, complete with a large cast and big budget. How-ever, the choice proved felicitous. Ultimately, Flynn and De Havilland appeared together in nine films.

With the exception of the sophisticated modern-day *Four's a Crowd*, they starred exclusively in swash-bucklers and westerns. In most of their films, Flynn rides a horse and sports a weapon, and De Havilland wears long skirts and worried looks. He's the adventurer, fight-ing pirates, Indians, or enemies of the British Empire. She's usually the spunky daughter or niece of a land baron, town elder, or diplomat; she's in love with Flynn but too proud to reveal her feelings.

He's not hard to love. Easily one of the most pho-togenic screen actors ever, Flynn had no peer when it came to costume adventures. He cut a fearless figure, fighting for justice and noble causes. Jack Warner, the head of Warner Brothers, noted: "As a matter of fact, (Flynn) had mediocre talent, but to the Walter Mittys of

Opposite:
In *Captain Blood*, Flynn is a doctor-turned-slave-turned-pirate
who is rescued on the auction block by De Havilland
and then returns the favor by dueling for her with
Basil Rathbone. "You're mine, do you understand me? Mine to
do with as I please," he tells her, and she doesn't protest.
Above:
Though this was standard dialogue for most of their movies,
the language veered more toward witty repartee in
their one and only contemporary film, *Four's a Crowd*,
in which Flynn looks none too comfortable.

the world, he was all the heroes in one magnificent, sexy, animal package. . . . Actor or no actor, he showered an audience with sparks when he laughed, when he fought and when he loved."

All of Flynn and De Havilland's films share a formula, particularly in terms of romance. Ironically, the stars spend little time together on screen. They meet in the first third of the film, right before he rides off to fulfill his destiny. Loving her is always dangerous for him because she's connected by blood, privilege, or rank to one of his enemies. Naturally, he scorns such danger, returning midway through the film to declare his love (and often climbing a trellis to embrace her on a balcony). Fearful, she sends him off, begging him to take care and come back to her. But in only four of their nine movies—*Captain Blood, The Adventures of Robin Hood, Dodge City,* and *Santa Fe Trail*—do they live happily ever after.

Though Flynn and De Havilland always fell in love (except in *The Charge of the Light Brigade,* in which De Havilland loved Flynn's brother), their films were hardly romances, at least not in the style of the great love stories of MGM. Warner Brothers made a different kind of love story than MGM, stressing adventure and action over sentiment.

Warner stars generally broke the traditional mold of Hollywood glamour. Actually, Flynn was odd man out in Warner's stable of stars, which included James Cagney, Edward G. Robinson, Paul Muni, and Humphrey Bogart. As writer Neal Gabler points out: "Only lithe, handsome Errol Flynn . . . could have qualified as a conventional romantic lead (his films were the most conventional Warner made). The others (Bogart, Cagney, and so on) were all decidedly smart and urban, small and explosive . . . and no one, not even Flynn, could possibly have been regarded as passive."

In their early films together, Flynn was so strong that De Havilland was relegated to doing little more than smiling and enduring his abandonment. She had become a much stronger presence and a more equal partner by the time they made their last major appearance together, in *They Died with Their Boots On.* But in all of their movies the love story remained secondary to his adventures. In fact, the relationship between Flynn and De Havilland never advanced the plot or caused the story to move in a particular direc-

Left and opposite: Flynn was hired for the lead in *Captain Blood* partly because he could wear long hair, ruffled shirts, and quirky hats and still look every inch the virile leading man.

tion. The element that counted most was action, of which there was always plenty. Considerable physical activity was required from Flynn's characters, and he was exactly the actor to provide it.

He was born in Tasmania in 1909, and before he reached Hollywood, he had already been an adventurer in real life. Rebellious and nonconformist, Flynn excelled in sports, especially boxing. He had staked a claim to a gold mine, bought a boat, and sailed the world for seven months. He had managed a tobacco plantation and had written a newspaper column about life in New Guinea. He had no acting experience, but because of his stunning good looks he was offered a part in an Australian film. Flynn enjoyed the work, and traveled to London in 1933 to pursue acting. By 1935, at the age of twenty-six, he had a contract at Warner Brothers and the lead in *Captain Blood*.

The daughter of a British patent attorney and a former actress, De Havilland was born in 1916 in Tokyo. (Her sister, the actress Joan Fontaine, was born a year later.) Her parents divorced, and in 1919 her mother brought the children to California. De Havilland acted in college, where she was seen by a talent scout and given a seven-year contract with Warner Brothers. Her big break came when she was teamed with Flynn.

Captain Blood now seems more dated than perhaps any other of Flynn's costumed adventure films. He was forced to recite such lines as: "I've resented you because you're beautiful and I'm a slave" and "No man should be late for his own hanging." The production seems tacky and the special effects were obviously done with miniatures, but the combination of prim and proper De Havilland and gallant, self-assured Flynn was a big bonus. In its day *Captain Blood* was such a success it made overnight stars of both actors. (She received five thousand marriage proposals from admirers of the film.) "Adventure on the high seas was clearly a hit with 1935 audiences . . . who responded to Flynn and De Havilland as to few other couples in screen adventure history," writes Peter Valenti. "Reviewers were extremely enthusiastic."

Captain Blood established Flynn's swashbuckler image and his rightful place as the successor to silent-screen stars Douglas Fairbanks, Sr., and John Barrymore. The *New York Post* declared: "If you haven't heard of Errol Flynn, it won't be long now. It is our prediction that Mr. Flynn will soon be as popular as the music of *Top Hat.*" The *Daily Mirror* called him "the first authentic matinee idol since Valentino." *Variety* insisted that the movie's only flaw was the lack of screen time for Flynn and De Havilland to court and spark. The *New York Times* called her "a lady of rapturous loveliness and well worth fighting for."

Captain Blood was also the second of nine Flynn movies, including *The Case of the Curious Bride* (where Flynn had a minor role), directed by Michael Curtiz, the legendary Hungarian filmmaker, who also directed such diverse classics as *Casablanca, Mildred Pierce,* and *Yankee Doodle Dandy.* Curtiz directed the next Flynn-De Havilland movie, *The Charge of the Light Brigade,* which was based on Alfred, Lord Tennyson's epic poem of the same title. Flynn had a hard time working with Curtiz, who was well known as a ruthless perfectionist. "I was to spend five miserable years with him," Flynn once said. "In each (picture) he tried to make all the scenes so realistic that my skin didn't seem to matter. Nothing delighted him more than real bloodshed."

Right, top and bottom:
"Why that valley is the valley of death!" exclaims a commandant, in a none-too-subtle reference to the Tennyson poem that was the inspiration for *The Charge of the Light Brigade.* Though the publicity stills promoted the two leads in a romantic embrace, in the movie De Havilland was actually in love with Flynn's brother, played by Patric Knowles, a Flynn clone who also costarred in *Four's a Crowd.*
Opposite:
Another famous costar, Ronald Reagan, appeared with De Havilland and Flynn in *Santa Fe Trail.* "They outnumber us three to one," whines Reagan before one of their many battles. "Well, if it makes you nervous, don't count," advises Flynn. Ironically, in this film Reagan played General George Custer.

Flynn's feelings for De Havilland helped get him through the ordeal. He later claimed that his "ardor for her made acting in that hard-to-make picture . . . bearable . . . all through it I fear I bothered Miss De Havilland in teasing ways—though I was really trying to display my affection." Typical of Flynn's displays was his placing of a dead snake in De Havilland's dressing room, among her underwear. De Havilland was repelled by Flynn's high-school antics but admitted: "I had a crush on him, and later found out he did for me. In fact, he proposed, but he was not divorced from (actress) Lili Damita so it was just as well that I had said no." Decades later, Bette Davis theorized in her memoirs that "it was Olivia de Havilland whom Flynn truly adored and who evaded him successfully in the end. I really believe that he was deeply in love with her."

Their next film together was probably their best, and again they were cast almost by accident. Warner Brothers had originally assigned James Cagney to the lead in *The Adventures of Robin Hood*, but Cagney walked off the set in a contract dispute, so Flynn was given the role. Since De Havilland had successfully played Flynn's leading lady in another costume epic, she was also assigned to this film. In fact, De Havilland did not especially enjoy working in action vehicles, and she eventually rebelled against Warner Brothers' forcing her into them.

Robin Hood was given the largest budget—a whooping $1.6 million—ever assigned a Warner picture, and was shot in vivid Technicolor. Under Curtiz's direction, the lavish production succeeded on every level. Flynn is particularly dashing, and De Havilland never looked lovelier than in Maid Marian's veils. She also shows a spark of independence here that was lacking in their first movies together. "I'm afraid of nothing, least of all you," she tells him. "It's a pity her manners don't match her looks," Flynn says of De Havilland, but he's naturally amused by the way she stands up to him. Later she warns: "Why, you speak treason." "Fluently," he replies with a grin.

De Havilland was unhappy with the movie, but years later, in Paris, she went to see the film and changed her mind. "Seeing *Robin Hood* after all those years made me realize how good all of our adventure films. were," De Havilland said, "and I wrote Errol that I was glad I had been in every scene of them . . . an

Opposite:
She was Maid Marian to his Robin Hood in the most famous swashbuckling adventure film ever made.
The Adventures of Robin Hood is perhaps the finest movie Flynn and De Havilland made together. He was perfectly cast as the dashing renegade, and she was allowed to show a little spunk for a change.
Above:
De Havilland had only a minor role in *The Private Lives of Elizabeth and Essex*, though, as usual, she played a woman in love with Flynn.

apology twenty years later. But I tore it up . . . deciding Errol would think I was silly."

Robin Hood was Flynn's crowning screen achievement, and by 1939 he was at the peak of his popularity. Wanting more serious work, he was pleased when Warner assigned him to make *Elizabeth the Queen* with Bette Davis. (The movie was released as *The Private Lives of Elizabeth and Essex*.)

Davis was not as thrilled to work with Flynn, as she demonstrated in terms of another, more famous, film. "In 1938 . . . Warners offered independent producer David O. Selznick full financing for his *Gone with the Wind* and 25 percent of the profits if he would use Flynn and Davis as Rhett and Scarlett in addition to De Havilland as Melanie. According to Davis and Jack L. Warner, Davis refused to have any part of a package deal involving Flynn, although she had always craved the role."

For her costar in *Elizabeth and Essex* Davis wanted Laurence Olivier, but Warner Brothers refused to pay for Olivier when they had Flynn under contract. Davis's reluctance to accept Flynn was a reflection of how Hollywood considered him little more than a pretty boy. Though he had wanted to prove himself in the film, he never stood a chance against an old war-horse like Davis. As usual, she acts everyone off the screen, including De Havilland, who appears as Davis's scheming lady-in-waiting and is also in love with Flynn. The film did little to bolster Flynn's reputation; in fact, Davis's extraordinary makeup, including her dramatically bald forehead, got more serious attention than Flynn's acting.

Flynn and De Havilland returned to their standard fare in *Santa Fe Trail* and *They Died with Their Boots On*, their last major film together and one of their best westerns. Here, De Havilland is her own woman, playing a gentle, but assertive Mrs. Custer to Flynn's reckless and headstrong general. It was one of the few times they played genuine equals. In their final scene together, he tells her: "Walking through life with you, Ma'am, has been a very gracious thing." He might well have been referring to their professional life together. Film critic David Shipman has suggested that "after De Havilland departed, Flynn was never quite the same."

De Havilland was anxious to have more important roles than those of the demure love interests in Flynn's adventure tales. She had shown her dramatic talent in *Gone with the Wind*, playing the gentle Melanie with a style and grace that earned her a first Oscar nomination. After her loan to Selznick, she demanded better roles and, for making such trouble, was suspended by Warner. When her contract expired, the studio claimed she still owed them the time she'd spent on suspension. She sued them and won a landmark decision, which set the limit of a studio-player contract at seven years, including periods of suspension.

Opposite, clockwise from top left:
Flynn comes a-courtin' De Havilland in *They Died with Their Boots On* (top left and right), *Dodge City*, and *Santa Fe Trail*.
Above:
Flynn and De Havilland in *Dodge City*. They were well suited to ride the range together, since he looked as if he really could handle a horse and she always seemed capable of handling him. It's no wonder, then, that Warner Brothers reteamed the couple in several shoot-'em-up dramas.

During the court battle, she was offscreen for three years, but she returned in 1946, winning an Academy Award for *To Each His Own*. Nominated many times, De Havilland again won the Oscar for Best Actress in 1949 for her splendid performance in *The Heiress*. Having divorced novelist Marcus Goodrich in 1946, she later married Pierre Galante, the editor of *Paris-Match*, and moved to Paris, where she still lives.

Flynn married three times. His first wife, Lili Damita, told a reporter in 1939: "I do not depend on Flynn for the things women usually expect of their husbands." Their marriage lasted seven years, and from that union came Flynn's only child.

Throughout Flynn's life, his flamboyant escapades, barroom brawls, and numerous liaisons made headlines. In 1942, he was tried for statutory rape. Even though acquitted, he was publicly humiliated during the trial when two girls, both underage, claimed to have had sexual relations with him. Warner Brothers was afraid that the trial would hurt Flynn at the box office, but the publicity only increased his fame. The expression "in like Flynn" was coined during that time.

By the mid '40s, the actor was thoroughly tired of his reputation both on and off the screen. Though he made more movies, his career was past its pinnacle. He had not been taken all that seriously before his trial, and after it he was treated with even less respect, especially by his peers. His first seven years in the movies were, by far, his best.

His discontent showed on screen, and by the end of the '40s his popularity had seriously waned. Always a heavy drinker and smoker, his experiments with narcotics became more and more evident in his appearance and performance. He left Hollywood and spent time in Europe and on his boat. He lost all his money on an ill-fated production of *William Tell.* In the late '50s, Olivia de Havilland recalled "an unhappy experience in Hollywood. A tall man kissed me on the back of the neck at a party and I whirled around in anger and said, 'Do I know you?' Then I realized it was Errol. He had changed so. His eyes were so sad. I had stared into them in enough movies to know his spirit was gone."

Flynn died of a heart attack at the age of fifty on October 14, 1959, in Canada. The coroner thought he was examining the ravaged body of a much older man. Yet Flynn managed to have the last word when his autobiography, *My Wicked, Wicked Ways,* was published later that year. In it he admitted to all his faults and foibles without apology. Interviewed at the time of Flynn's death, De Havilland was quoted as saying: "He was a charming and magnetic man, but so tormented. I don't know about what, but tormented." Jack Warner said that Flynn "was one of the most charming and tragic men I have known."

The legend of Errol Flynn still survives. It has been suggested that Peter O'Toole modeled his performance in *My Favorite Year* (1982) after Flynn. O'Toole plays a flamboyant aging film star who, when accused of being drunk, shouts: "If I were plastered, could I do this?" and then somersaults across a conference table. It was a gesture worthy of Flynn.

In 1991, Kevin Costner reprised the role of Robin Hood in a $60-million remake of the tale. As well, Tracey Ullman appeared in *The Big Love,* a one-woman show about the life of Beverly Aadland, Errol Flynn's last lover (and the last in a string of jailbait liaisons). The show was based on the "tell-all" best-seller by Florence Aadland, Beverly's mother.

Since Flynn's death, many rumors about him have circulated, including tales of his alleged association with Nazis during World War II and of his flirtation with homosexuality. Little substantial proof exists to verify either of these claims, but the fact that Flynn still generates so much public interest thirty years after his death is testament to the legacy of his screen performances.

TYPICAL LOVE SCENE
Errol Flynn and Olivia de Havilland

Errol Flynn and Olivia de Havilland played
the same love scene in nearly every one of their films.
Note the similarity between these two scenes:

DE HAVILLAND: But you can still save yourself, please, for my sake.

FLYNN: For your sake? What do you mean: for your sake? Isn't it true that you hate me?

DE HAVILLAND: Hate you?

FLYNN: Or is it that you love me?

DE HAVILLAND: I'll hide you, and then tonight, after dark, I'll find some way. . . .

FLYNN: You love me. Don't you? Don't you?

DE HAVILLAND: Whom else would I love?

FLYNN: You love me! Lord Willoughby, she loves me! She loves me!

CAPTAIN BLOOD

FLYNN: You're in love with me. You are, aren't you? 'Cause I'm in love with you, terribly. That's why I came, I had to see you again.

DE HAVILLAND: You must go at once, and I don't love you. . . .

FLYNN: Very well, then. I'll go. This is rather unfriendly of you, exposing me to my enemies.

DE HAVILLAND: Robin, please.

FLYNN: Then you do love me. Don't you? Don't you?

DE HAVILLAND: You know I do.

FLYNN: Well, then, that's different.

THE ADVENTURES OF ROBIN HOOD

FILMOGRAPHY

Captain Blood (1935)
The Charge of the Light Brigade (1936)
The Adventures of Robin Hood (1938)
Four's a Crowd (1938)
Dodge City (1939)

The Private Lives of Elizabeth and Essex (1939)
Santa Fe Trail (1940)
They Died with Their Boots On (1941)
Thank Your Lucky Stars (1943) (guest appearances)

good clean fun
GARLAND & ROONEY

"We just do a little hugging and kissing, Dad.
I mean, good, clean fun, just like me and Polly."

Mickey Rooney and Lewis Stone, LOVE FINDS ANDY HARDY (1938)

Judy Garland and Mickey Rooney were the quintessential teenagers of the late '30s and early '40s. The kids next door, they were devoted to their parents, loyal to their friends, full of life, and bursting with energy. Sure, they suffered teenage angst, but it was always over getting a first kiss or raising thirty dollars to buy a car. If real life seemed simpler back then, then life in these movies seemed simpleminded.

As a team, Garland and Rooney made two types of movies: inspirational family entertainment, à la Andy Hardy, and "let's-put-on-a-show" musicals. They were magical in both formulas, complementing each other's styles and talents. He was brash and vibrant; she was wistful and shy. He often made her laugh; she always got him out of a jam.

Their equality has been noted by movie critic David Shipman: "Contemporary critics thought he overshadowed her, but there is something winning in her work—a directness of emotion in her usually unspoken crush on him and her sad little songs, and the enforced precocity of her handling of the more typical peppy songs."

The two child stars came from remarkably similar backgrounds. Both were born to vaudeville parents and made their stage debuts as toddlers. Born Frances Gumm in 1922, she was three years old when she first appeared with her sisters as part of the "Gumm Sisters Kiddie Act." Billed as "the little girl with the great big voice," she auditioned at the age of thirteen for Louis B. Mayer, and was given a contract without a screen test. She made several shorts and appeared in a supporting role before making a real hit when she sang "Dear Mr. Gable" to a photograph of the star in *Broadway*

Opposite:
Judy Garland and Mickey Rooney didn't really become a bona fide screen couple until their second feature,
Love Finds Andy Hardy.
Above:
Garland got star billing for the first time in
Thoroughbreds Don't Cry, which costarred
Ronald Sinclair and Rooney, who was well-cast as
"the pluckiest jockey on the track."

Melody of 1938. Garland costarred with Rooney for the first time in *Thoroughbreds Don't Cry.*

By then Rooney was already a star. Born Joe Yule, Jr., he was barely two years old when he appeared on stage. At the age of six, he worked in his first silent film, and between 1927 and 1933 he appeared in more than fifty two-reelers under the name Mickey McGuire. He became Mickey Rooney in 1932, when he was twelve years old, and made his mark as Puck in *A Midsummer Night's Dream* before being offered his first *Andy Hardy* movie.

The *Andy Hardy* movies made up one of the most successful series ever. After the first one, *A Family Affair,* the public was completely hooked and clamored for more. MGM was more than happy to oblige. The series was a passion of Louis B. Mayer's, and he supervised every detail. "When you look at *Andy Hardy* pictures," said Mayer's grandson Danny Selznick, "you think of a man who had a very strong morality—a kind of strait-laced morality. . . . These were pictures in which children learned from their parents. And that was a very strong reflection of Louis B. Mayer."

Mayer also believed that playing Andy Hardy gave Rooney a moral obligation. Director-writer Billy Wilder recalled being on the MGM lot one day: "We looked out the window because there was screaming going on, and Louis B. Mayer held Mickey Rooney by the lapel. He says, 'You're Andy Hardy! You're the United States! You're the Stars and Stripes. Behave yourself! You're a symbol!'" Mayer's faith in Andy Hardy proved itself at the box office. In 1938 *Love Finds Andy Hardy* outgrossed films that cost ten times as much.

Today, the series seems like an obvious forerunner of many successful television sitcoms. Certainly, the formula was the same: good, old-fashioned family values and homespun wisdom. Dad, played by Lewis Stone, is wise and strong. "The next ten years of my life are the best," Andy tells Judge Hardy in *Life Begins for Andy Hardy.* "The next ten years of anybody's life are the best," the Judge replies sagely. Fay Holden,

Left, top and bottom:
Love Finds Andy Hardy **was the fourth in the**
Andy Hardy **series but the first to costar Judy Garland.**
Although Garland, Rooney, and Lana Turner
became world-famous, in real life they
were teenagers who had to do their homework
between takes.

as Andy's mom, is kind and understanding, worrying about her family and her chocolate pudding with equal energy.

And that boy, Andy, was always getting into mischief, usually when he got too big for his britches. "You and trouble just naturally gravitate towards one another," Garland tells him in *Andy Hardy Meets Debutante*.

Garland played Betsy Booth to Rooney's Andy. This "poor, little rich girl" from New York City frequently visited her grandmother, who lived next door to the Hardys in the all-American town of Carvel. In *Love Finds Andy Hardy*, Garland is supposed to be twelve (she was

actually sixteen) to Rooney's sixteen (he was eighteen), and, consequently, he considers her much too young to be taken seriously. (The "love" of the title was actually Lana Turner.) In fact, Rooney and Garland never find romance in the *Andy Hardy* movies. He always has another girlfriend, someone older, but never wiser or truer, than Garland.

Pining away for him, little Judy always wishes she looked older. "Gosh, sometimes, I wish a girl could have her face lifted upside down," she says in *Life Begins for Andy Hardy*. And she's despondent over her lack of glamour. "I'll never be able to get a man, much less hold him. No glamour (she looks down at her chest). . . . No glamour at all," she wails in *Love Finds Andy Hardy*.

Always a true friend, Garland helps solve his problems with the other girls in his life. In *Love Finds Andy Hardy*, she squares him with his girl, Polly (Ann Rutherford). In *Andy Hardy Meets Debutante*, Garland introduces him to the deb of the title, who is played by Diana Lewis (in real life, the future Mrs. William Powell.) In *Life Begins for Andy Hardy*, Garland saves Rooney from the clutches of a ruthless New York glamour girl. And what reward does Garland get from Rooney? "You couldn't have done more for me if you'd been an adult my own age," he tells her in *Debutante*.

Although the series was popular before (and after) Garland was in it, *Life Begins for Andy Hardy*, her third and last *Hardy* movie, was the most successful of the sixteen films. The series seemed like the goose that laid the golden egg, at least until *Love Laughs at Andy Hardy*, which bombed in 1946. MGM tried once more in 1958, bringing back the cast (again without Garland) for *Andy Hardy Comes Home*. The box-office results were disastrous, and Andy Hardy was permanently shelved.

Though Garland could never get Rooney to treat her as a girlfriend in the *Andy Hardy* movies, she was on somewhat more equal footing with him in their hectic musicals. The first, and decidedly the best, was *Babes in Arms* (1939), which set the formula for all their future musicals. "Are you kids willing to stick together and pull yourself out of a hole?" Rooney asks the neighborhood kids. "I've got an idea. Our folks think we're babes in arms, huh? Well, we'll show them whether we're babes in arms or not. I'm going to write a show for us, and put it on right here in Seaport. . . . We'll get every kid in this town on our side, and we'll start right now. What do you

Left, top and bottom:
To impress his friends, Rooney pretends to have a society girlfriend in *Andy Hardy Meets Debutante*, and Garland is the only one who can help him save face. "Sometimes a woman's intuition is better than a man's brains," says budding feminist Garland. The most entertaining aspect of this *Hardy* film is Garland's rendition of such songs as "I'm Nobody's Baby Now."

Above and right:
Babes in Arms was the first of the Garland-Rooney "let's-put-on-a-show" musicals. The premise is a bit far-fetched, but these two major talents knew how to deliver a show, singing and dancing to such classics as "Where or When," " I Cried for You," and "God's Country."

say?" Almost identical dialogue would be spoken by Rooney in *Strike Up the Band, Babes on Broadway,* and *Girl Crazy.*

Though Garland is more mature in the musicals, she still plays a girl haunted by her lack of glamour. "I know I'm no glamour girl . . . but maybe someday you'll realize that glamour isn't the only thing in this world," she says to a photo of Rooney in *Babes in Arms.* Garland was probably forced to play this kind of role because MGM never treated her as a great beauty. Her face wasn't photogenic in the style of such rivals for Andy

Opposite:
Strike Up the Band re-grouped much of the cast from
Babes in Arms for another version of the same story.
"We'll put on a show; that'll be different," claims Rooney.
Yeah, right. Lovelorn yet again, Garland sings
"Our Love Affair," "I Ain't Got Nobody," and "Do the Conga."

This page, clockwise from top left:
In *Babes on Broadway* Rooney plays Cyrano in a show
he and Garland produce to save the orphans
of a settlement house.

In *Girl Crazy* they stage an all-singing, all-dancing rodeo to
rescue their private school from bankruptcy. Though the
premise by now fairly creaked with wear and tear, audiences
were more than compensated by the Gershwin score, which
included "Embraceable You," "But Not for Me,"
and "I Got Rhythm."

Girl Crazy was the final Rooney-Garland film, although they
both made guest appearances in the musical review
Thousands Cheer, and Rooney hosted a feature appearance
by Garland in *Words and Music,* where this behind-the-scenes
publicity still with a very young Liza Minnelli was taken.

Hardy's affections as Lana Turner and Ann Rutherford. And there was Garland's weight problem, which was as publicized then as Oprah Winfrey's diets are today.

It's well known that the studio, and Mayer in particular, was responsible for providing the adolescent Garland with diet pills. To compensate for the uppers, she was given sleeping pills, and so developed a debilitating addiction to prescription drugs. It's true that her body did not photograph well. In many of her films, she looks either too plump or just plain gawky. As she says in *Babes in Arms:* "I might be good looking myself when I grow out of this ugly-duckling stage." However, Garland *was* beautiful, perhaps not in the MGM mold of high cheekbones and tiny waistlines, but beautiful nonetheless, with doelike eyes and a gentle mouth.

In any case, even the studio saw that any of her supposed physical shortcomings quickly vanished the moment she began to sing. That voice more than compensated for any lack of glamour. Garland sang with her whole heart and always seemed to be giving herself away in a performance. She was beautiful to hear and to watch.

Though Rooney couldn't sing as well as Garland (and who could?), he had other talents to match hers. He brought tremendous youthful energy and exuberance to the screen. Hair flying, legs flapping, arms swinging, he generated vitality in his production numbers and, smiling all the way, seemed to be having a great time. He took pratfalls and cried on cue, and when he was happy no one could be happier. He had a wonderful flair for impersonations, doing Clark Gable and Lionel Barrymore in at least three of his movies with Garland. In *Babes on Broadway,* he cavorted outrageously as Carmen Miranda.

When that film opened at Radio City Music Hall in 1942, more than 133,000 people flocked to see it in the first five days. It was followed by another Garland-Rooney smash hit, *Girl Crazy.* Both performers were at the peak of their careers. She had received worldwide acclaim and a special Oscar for her performance as Dorothy in *The Wizard of Oz.* He was the number one box-office attraction in both the United States and Britain. He was twenty-two years old, she twenty, and, although they would have occasional triumphs in the years to come, for the most part, their best days were behind them.

Ironically, both these former child stars, who had made their living playing happy teenagers, had troubled adult lives. By the late '40s, Rooney could barely find work. At the end of *Life Begins for Andy Hardy* he exclaims: "I guess I'll never grow up!" The sentiment haunted his career. Typecast as a perennial teenager, he couldn't get hired as an adult actor. Although he earned more than $12 million as a young man, Rooney went bankrupt in 1962. Much of his money had been consumed by alimony payments, since he had married eight times. In 1963, Rooney was reunited with Garland on her television show. "This is the love of my life," he told the audience. "There isn't an adjective in the world to express my love for Judy." Rooney has remained active in the past two decades, working on TV and in nightclubs.

Plagued by her addiction to pills and her paralyzing insecurity, Garland was fired by MGM in 1950. After fifteen years at the top, at the age of twenty-eight, it looked as if she was finished in show business. She divorced her second husband, Vincente Minnelli, father of her now-famous daughter, Liza, in 1951. The same year, she performed in a major concert tour. She married Sid Luft in 1952 and then gave birth to a second daughter, Lorna. With the help of Luft, she rejuvenated her popularity in a remake of the film *A Star Is Born,* but her triumph was cut short by many well-publicized personal problems.

The papers continually reported stories of her lawsuits, nervous breakdowns, and suicide attempts. On June 22, 1969, she was found dead from an overdose of barbiturates. The coroner said her death was accidental, but Ray Bolger, the Scarecrow in *The Wizard of Oz,* commented: "She just plain wore out." Ironically, Garland was both the greatest achievement of the studio system at MGM—and its most tragic victim.

TYPICAL LOVE SCENE
Judy Garland and Mickey Rooney

Actually, Garland and Rooney had no typical love scenes, as she was rarely his love interest. Usually, she was just a friend. In *Babes on Broadway*, though, MGM finally allowed them to have a love scene. Well, almost a love scene. Call it a good, clean love scene.

They meet in a drugstore, and then they get involved in putting on a show to help the orphans of the settlement house where Garland works. She's been goofy over him from the start, but in typical Garland-Rooney fashion he's been too busy worrying about the show to notice her until they have an argument. He apologizes, and then realizes he actually loves her.

MICKEY: I've got a couple of words I want to say to you . . . well, really three.

JUDY: Go ahead and say them, and get them over with.

MICKEY: Ohhhh, I could say I love you, just like all the rest of them.

JUDY: That's still good, you know.

MICKEY: But it wouldn't tell you what I really mean.

JUDY: Well, I'll settle for it.

MICKEY: Oh, no. You're not going to talk me out of my love scene. Were you ever in a rainstorm, and you felt like the only person in the world that wasn't getting wet? Did you ever look up and see a full moon, and it only looked like a half-moon to you 'cause you were looking at it alone? Did you ever find someone, and all of a sudden you felt like you were taking off? Right out into space, like a propeller going round and round and round; thirty thousand revolutions a minute, and there wasn't any landing fields left in the world?

JUDY: Uh, huh. I've had that feeling, and it all started in a drugstore.

MICKEY: Penny.

JUDY: Yeah. (*They kiss.*) Tommy.

MICKEY: Oh, isn't it wonderful what you can find these days in a drugstore! Oh gosh!

FILMOGRAPHY

Thoroughbreds Don't Cry (1937)
Love Finds Andy Hardy (1938)
Babes in Arms (1939)
Andy Hardy Meets Debutante (1940)

Strike Up the Band (1940)
Life Begins for Andy Hardy (1941)
Babes on Broadway (1941)
Girl Crazy (1943)

Thousands Cheer (1943) (guest appearances)
Words and Music (1948) (Rooney hosted, Garland made a guest appearance)

enduring love
GARSON & PIDGEON

"It's been a rather perfect marriage."

Greer Garson, THE MINIVER STORY (1950)

An ideal screen couple, Greer Garson and Walter Pidgeon looked as if they were made for each other. Both tall and statuesque, they exuded a kind of upper-class British elegance and style. She was lovely, with red hair, green eyes, and milky white skin. He was handsome, with dark hair, blue eyes, and a distinguished brow. In many of their movies, they meet as young adults and then grow old together. No screen couple aged with more grace and dignity than did Garson and Pidgeon.

Totally believable as a devoted, long-married couple, they seemed at ease with each other. When she needed to take his arm, it was always available to her. Occasionally they argued, but never about their love for one another. They respected each other and were true equals, intellectually in *Madame Curie,* compassionately in *Blossoms in the Dust,* professionally in *Mrs. Parkington,* and patriotically in *Mrs. Miniver.*

On screen they displayed a genuine affection. The most frequently uttered word in any Garson-Pidgeon movie is "darling." They also understood each other. In *Mrs. Miniver,* when Pidgeon says "You left the dressing room light on again," it's with an adroit mixture of annoyance and humor which comes from a loving heart.

In 1938 Louis B. Mayer discovered Greer Garson on a London stage. The Irish-born beauty had given up a steady job in advertising to seek her fame in the theater. She had appeared in numerous plays, and

Opposite:
As a screen couple, Greer Garson and Walter Pidgeon were perfect together, as evidenced in this still from their most famous movie, *Mrs. Miniver.* He was stunningly handsome, and she was one of the most gorgeous women in Hollywood; no wonder they looked so good together on screen!

because of her demeanor was known in the West End as the "Duchess of Garson." But Mayer obviously appreciated her style. He arrived backstage one night to offer her a contract, and she left for Hollywood almost immediately.

For a year, she was unable to get work as no one at MGM knew what to do with her refined English looks. She was too tall for most leading men, and her face had an odd bone structure. She sported tweed skirts and flat heels, and wore her hair pulled back severely, not at all like the traditional MGM movie queens. The studio tested her for many different projects but didn't cast her in anything. The lack of attention, especially after she'd been the toast of London, made Garson desperately unhappy, and she talked about returning to England.

Then, one day, director Sam Wood was casting *Goodbye, Mr. Chips* (1939). Garson wasn't considered until, by accident, one of her early screen tests was flashed on screen. In it, she appeared without the benefit of makeup and dressed in her street clothes, but Wood was charmed by her unique and natural beauty. The phenomenal success of the film won Garson international acclaim and an Oscar nomination. MGM received scores of letters from fans demanding to see her again.

She made her first film with Pidgeon in 1941. *Blossoms in the Dust* was a somewhat fictionalized biography of child welfare worker Edna Gladney, who founded the Texas Children's Home and Society at the turn of the century. Garson played Gladney, a willful, determined woman who says that "every child born into this world belongs to the whole human race." Pidgeon was the perfect match for such a strong female lead. Though he was never as commanding on screen as Gable or

A slick tear-jerker, *Blossoms in the Dust*
begins with numerous family tragedies for Garson and Pidgeon;
the adorable children in its cast,
such as this young extra playing a destitute orphan,
add to the melodrama.

Tracy, his gentlemanly style and quiet reserve made him a good partner for an imposing leading lady. Garson could fall into his arms whenever tragedy struck, which it did with alarming frequency in *Blossoms in the Dust*.

In the first reel of the film, Garson's sister commits suicide, and her young child dies in an accident. Shortly thereafter, Pidgeon goes bankrupt, Garson takes in a slew of orphans, and she has to beg money for milk. Then, Pidgeon dies suddenly. Finally, Garson is forced to give up the one child she has nursed and loved for years. Like all of the Garson-Pidgeon movies, *Blossoms* has a strong message to deliver. In one climactic scene, Garson addresses a somewhat hostile Texas Senate, pleading for the passage of a bill to protect adopted children. "There are no illegitimate children, there are only illegitimate parents," she cries, emerging triumphant in the end.

Blossoms solidified Garson's status as a bona fide star, establishing her and Pidgeon as a team of enduring value to MGM. The *New York Times* glorified Garson as "a vision of loveliness with her red hair delicately framing her expressive face. . . . (She) conveys through the picture a conviction of sincerity and sensitivity." *Time* magazine spoke of "an eloquent performance by Miss Garson, whose green eyes, red hair and alabaster complexion make her a Technicolor natural." For her work in that movie, Garson was nominated for a second Oscar (though Joan Fontaine won for her performance in *Suspicion*.)

Garson's star at MGM was rising rapidly; she became one of Mayer's favorite actresses. Actually, she couldn't have picked a better time to be working at the studio. The departure of Greta Garbo, Norma Shearer, and Joan Crawford left a void that Garson was well suited to fill. She was also lucky in that Pidgeon, at the age of forty-four, was available for work, since most of the younger actors in Hollywood were off to war at the time.

Like Garson, Pidgeon began his career on the stage, frequently starring in musicals. He worked at Universal until MGM bought his contract in 1937 and put him in *Saratoga* with Jean Harlow. The part helped boost his career, and by the end of 1938 he had appeared in eleven films. Known for his good looks, he was typecast as a leading man who wore clothes well and moved easily through society. One columnist called Pidgeon "beyond any question the handsomest man in Hollywood." His acting talent was another matter. Critic James Agate once described Pidgeon as "that handsome piece of screen furniture." Wanting to prove himself as an actor, Pidgeon asked for more substantial work, which he got in such films as *How*

Opposite:
Blossoms in the Dust was the first Garson-Pidgeon movie, and it was evident from the start that they were not only compatible but meant for each other. The moment they meet in this film (and in many of their subsequent movies) he declares his intention to marry her. Part of the Garson-Pidgeon magic was making love at first sight seem not only possible, but inevitable.

Above:
In some ways, Garson and Pidgeon were the British equivalents of Tracy and Hepburn; without the brilliant wit, perhaps,
but certainly they projected the same sense of genuine affection, admiration, and respect that made Tracy and Hepburn seem so
comfortable together on the big screen. Without question, *Mrs. Miniver* is the ultimate example of how well Garson and Pidgeon
worked together as a screen couple. They play a happily married couple who endure the hardships of war while continually
complimenting each other. "You're quite a beautiful woman," he tells her. "If you think so, darling," she modestly replies. Yes,
they truly love each other— even though, like all Hollywood couples, they sleep in separate beds.
Opposite:
Though they were always well-matched in their movies, Garson and Pidgeon were never more equal
than in *Madame Curie*. She's as smart as he and works just as hard, maybe harder.

Green Was My Valley. Perhaps, though, his greatest role was as Garson's loving husband in *Mrs. Miniver*.

Being a true Anglophile, Louis B. Mayer had bought the screen rights to the Miniver tale. He had had Norma Shearer in mind for the lead, but she refused to play the mother of a teenager, fearing it would damage her image. So, encouraged by the success of *Blossoms in the Dust*, Mayer selected Garson for the role. She also had reservations about playing an older wom-an, but was finally persuaded to accept the role. (Ironically, Garson would later marry Richard Ney, the young man who played her son in the film.) From the beginning, it was clear that the movie had a message to deliver. Producer Sidney Franklin had accepted the *Mrs. Miniver* project because he "had the notion that someone should make a tribute, a salute to England, which was battling for its life. Suddenly, I realized I should be the someone."

In *Madame Curie* the ever-persistent Garson pushes Pidgeon to continue their experiments even after he wants to quit, right up until the climactic moment when they are actually able to see the luminescent radium for the first time.

Mrs. Miniver proved to be one of the most influential and important films made in Hollywood during the war. An upper-middle-class couple with three children and a lovely home, the Minivers exemplified the indomitable British spirit, reading *Alice in Wonderland* to their children as bombs dropped overhead. Their oldest son went off to war while they built a bomb shelter in the back yard and helped with the war effort. They displayed all the right values and were completely

When they first meet in *Madame Curie*, Pidgeon is an awkward, people-shy scientist who believes that women shouldn't be allowed in the lab. Garson quickly changes his attitude. Though she is absolutely beautiful, she's also all business, interested only in physics and mathematics. Her technical talk turns him on, and he takes to whistling in the lab. Soon, he invites her to his parent's house for the weekend and then proposes marriage. But their relationship is not all romance. Once they marry, they begin their tedious experiments, which eventually lead to the discovery of radium.

In *Mrs. Parkington* wealthy Pidgeon meets poor but lovely Garson in a boarding house, falls madly in love, and whisks her off to his fabulous mansion. If that ain't movie heaven, what is?

devoted to family, church, and community. "What makes *Mrs. Miniver* work as super-screen entertainment and tangentially as allied propaganda is the solidarity of the Miniver family in the war crisis," writes James Parrish. Although they suffered several tragedies, such as the death of their daughter-in-law (Teresa Wright), the Minivers—like England—managed to survive, sending a message the world wanted and needed in those troubled times. Winston Churchill said that *Mrs. Miniver* did more for the British war effort than a fleet of destroyers.

The movie also made box-office history. In the first twenty-five days of its run at Radio City Music Hall, more than half a million people bought tickets, sales exceeding those of *The Philadelphia Story,* the previous record holder. *Mrs. Miniver* won six Academy Awards, including those for Best Picture, Best Actress, and Best Director. Ironically, director William Wyler was unavailable to accept his award at the ceremony, as he was flying a bombing run over Germany at the time.

The landmark role of Mrs. Miniver cemented Garson's screen image as a wife and mother of resolute courage and dedication. She would be cast in the same kind of role again and again, as often as not with Pidgeon by her side. Mayer probably never considered anyone else to play the lead in *Madame Curie.* Based on Éve Curie's biography of her mother, the film detailed the marriage of Pierre and Marie Curie and their struggle to discover radium. The *New York Times* said: "Greer Garson and Walter Pidgeon are ideal in the leading roles, ideal, that is, to the necessity of creating warm characters. Miss Garson, the invariable patrician, plays with that gentle, wistful grace which makes her a glowing representation of feminine nobility and charm. And Mr. Pidgeon is magnificently modest and slyly masculine as the preoccupied professor whom she loves."

They played the Curies according to the formula that had made them popular as a team. Though Marie Curie was Polish and Pierre was French, both actors spoke with British accents. The film was marred by several conventional Hollywood ploys, such as an idyllic bicycle trip through the countryside and endless scenes of the couple struggling nobly side by side in the lab. Despite these flaws, Garson and Pidgeon were never more equal than in this movie.

In the beginning of the film Pidgeon says: "Women and science are incompatible. No true scientist can have anything to do with a woman." Of course, Garson proves him wrong. She's as smart and as dedicated as he, perhaps even more so. He wants to give up after hundreds of experiments, but she convinces him to continue. When he dies in an accident, she finds the strength to carry on their work for the next twenty-five years. At the end of the film, she delivers one of her typical rousing speeches, this time to her fellow researchers at the University of Paris. "You, take the torch of knowledge, and behold the palace of the future," she tells her colleagues. It was a tour-de-force performance for Garson, and James Agate wrote: "I am inclined to think the time has come to recognize Greer Garson as the next best film actress to Bette Davis."

A generational tale that hinged on the relationship between a married couple, *Mrs. Parkington* continued the Garson-Pidgeon tradition. Garson ages from about nineteen to eighty years old, beginning as a maid in a boardinghouse and becoming the matriarch of a wealthy society family. Based on Louis Bromfield's best-

Left: (top and bottom)
Garson and Pidgeon age beautifully in *Mrs. Parkington*.
Above:
The fittingly titled *Julia Misbehaves* was a definite mistake,
casting Garson as a mad-cap dancer who sings, smokes,
shows off her legs, and sports a black beauty mark on her chin.
Pidgeon is forced to perform slapstick comedy. The movie was
a flop, perhaps because Garson and Pidgeon were so miscast.
Overleaf:
A decidedly photogenic moment from *The Miniver Story*.

seller, the movie was a box-office smash. Today, the flashback-infested footage is still serviceable, though it quickly wears thin.

However, Garson and Pidgeon were really in trouble when they abandoned their formula all together. *Julia Misbehaves* was perhaps their greatest folly. Going against her refined screen image, Garson plays a madcap dance hall performer who has given up her baby daughter after a brief marriage to highbrow Pidgeon. But she returns to the ancestral estate for the marriage of her daughter, played by Elizabeth Taylor. The film suffers from an acute case of forced gaiety; the acting is strained in almost every scene.

In 1950 MGM attempted to revive the success of the Minivers in *The Miniver Story*. Without the war as background, the magic is clearly gone. Garson spends the entire film dying of an unidentified disease, the fatal Hollywood kind, from which the patient has six months to live but looks absolutely gorgeous and healthy in every shot.

Left:
That Forsyte Woman followed the fiasco of *Julia Misbehaves*.
Above:
Attempting to revive their popularity, Garson and Pidgeon starred in *The Miniver Story*, which proved to be a weak sequel to the smash hit *Mrs. Miniver*.

In 1953, Garson and Pidgeon appeared together for the last time, in *Scandal at Scourie*, a tedious film about small-town politics and Catholic-Protestant antagonism. The film was a failure as well as an ignominious end to a remarkable screen partnership.

Pidgeon was once quoted as saying: "Favorite pictures? Any of the ones with Greer Garson." In his long career, he appeared in more than one hundred films. He died in 1984, at the age of eighty-six.

Garson's career in Hollywood spanned about fifteen years, but her most productive time was between 1939 and 1945. She begged out of her MGM contract in 1954, and, even though good movie roles were scarce for her after 1945, she garnered a total of seven Oscar nominations, a fitting tribute to her talent. She lives in retirement in Santa Fe, New Mexico, with her third husband, Elijah Fogelson.

As a couple Garson and Pidgeon came to symbolize enduring love, embodying a multitude of domestic virtues for their time. Though the Garson-Pidgeon movies may seem dated and melodramatic, they were much beloved in their day. As James Parrish points out: "Elders who sigh, 'They don't make movies like that anymore,' can recall when the promise of a new Garson-Pidgeon feature meant a leisurely, plush excursion into a world of nobility, gentility, and tear-inducing emotions, refinements long gone."

As a screen couple, Garson and Pidgeon came full circle with their last film, *Scandal at Scourie*. Ironically, it concerned the problems of placing orphans for adoption, echoing the theme of *Blossoms in the Dust*, their first movie together.

FILMOGRAPHY
Greer Garson and Walter Pidgeon

Blossoms in the Dust (1941)
Mrs. Miniver (1942)
The Youngest Profession (1943)
    (guest appearance)
Madame Curie (1943)

Mrs. Parkington (1944)
Julia Misbehaves (1948)
That Forsyte Woman (1949)
The Miniver Story (1950)
Scandal at Scourie (1953)

TYPICAL LOVE SCENE
Greer Garson and Walter Pidgeon

Garson and Pidgeon were always in love, but that was never the focal point of their film partnership. Their movies always had a moral, a message, or a lesson to deliver. Perhaps the most emotional moment of any Garson-Pidgeon movie was the vicar's eulogy from *Mrs. Miniver.* The speech was so stirring that President Roosevelt had leaflets of it air-dropped over Europe. Certainly, the speech best exemplified the most compelling element of any Garson-Pidgeon movie.

"We in this quiet corner of England have suffered the loss of friends very dear to us. Some, close to the church. . . .

"And our hearts go out in sympathy to the two families who share the cruel loss of a young girl who was married at this altar only two weeks ago. The homes of many of us have been destroyed, and the lives of young and old have been taken. There is scarcely a household that hasn't been struck to the heart.

"And why? Surely you must have asked yourself this question. Why, in all conscience, should these be the ones to suffer? Children, old people, a young girl at the height of her loveliness. Why these? Are these our soldiers? Are these our fighters? Why should they be sacrificed?

"I shall tell you why. Because this is not only a war of soldiers in uniform. It is a war of the people—all of the people—and it must be fought not only on the battlefield, but in the cities and in the villages, in the factories and on the farms, in the home and in the heart of every man, woman, and child who loves freedom. Well, we have buried our dead, but we shall not forget them. Instead, they will inspire us with unbearable determination to free ourselves and those who come after us from the tyranny and terror that threatens to strike us down.

"This is the people's war! It is our war! We are the fighters! Fight it then! Fight it with all that is in us! And may God defend the right!"

PART TWO

lovers offscreen

BOGART & BACALL

"The trouble with Bogart is that he thinks he's Bogart."

DAVE CHASEN, Restaurateur

In *Play It Again, Sam,* Woody Allen pays homage to Humphrey Bogart. "You know who's not insecure? Bogie," he tells Diane Keaton. When she remarks that Allen is setting too high a standard for himself, he replies: "Well, look, if I'm going to identify, who am I going to pick? My rabbi? I mean, Bogart's a perfect image."

He was to millions of others, too, although he was the most unlikely of heroes. Bogart's looks, for instance, were less than classic. He was short, with a scrawny body, beady eyes, and a receding hairline. Wounded in World War I, his upper lip was paralyzed; hence, his face was molded into a perpetual scowl and he also spoke with a lisp.

In *Dark Passage*, a plastic surgeon gives Bogie the once over and says of that famous face, "You look as if you've lived," which is as kind and as apt a description of Bogart as any ever written.

He looked like a hood and was cast as one on stage in *The Petrified Forest.* The movie version of this play launched his career at Warner Brothers, where he played a succession of gangsters. "In my first thirty-four pictures," Bogart told writer George Frazier, "I was shot twelve times, electrocuted or hanged in eight and I was a jailbird in nine. . . . I played more scenes writhing around on the floor than I did standing up."

The typecasting grated on Bogie's nerves. "I'm sick to death of being a one-dimensional character," he said to another reporter. "I'm just a guy in a tight suit

Opposite:
"I'm hard to get," Bacall tells Bogart in *To Have and Have Not,* "all you have to do is ask." Her sultry, sensuous advances startle, amuse, and entice Bogart, who knows a classy dame when one falls into his lap.

and a snap-brim hat. I have no function except to carry the plot and get killed."

On the Warner lot, Bogie had to compete with other tough-guy actors, such as Edward G. Robinson, James Cagney, and Paul Muni. Bogie was mostly assigned to the movies his coworkers had rejected. His break came in 1941, when he was cast in *High Sierra* after both Paul Muni and George Raft turned down the role. Bogart gave one of his best performances as a weary, aging gangster who wanted to retire. The same year he played Sam Spade in the near-perfect *Maltese Falcon.* In 1942, after George Raft had turned down the part, Bogart was cast opposite Ingrid Bergman in *Casablanca,* cementing his reputation as one of the best actors in American movies. (In the same film, Ronald Reagan was originally cast in Paul Henreid's role as Bergman's husband.) But it wasn't until Bogart met Lauren Bacall that he also became one of Hollywood's most popular sex symbols.

Bacall was discovered on the cover of *Harper's Bazaar* in March 1943 by the wife of director Howard Hawks, who was looking for a new girl to play opposite Bogart in *To Have and Have Not.* Although Bacall was only nineteen years old and totally inexperienced, a screen test proved her highly photogenic. The tall, slim, sultry blonde had "the look." Before she had ever appeared on screen, Hawks signed her to a personal contract and then sold fifty percent to Warner Brothers, so the studio would finance *To Have and Have Not.*

Bogie and Bacall met while filming *To Have and Have Not,* and the interaction between them set a new precedent in films. Though he plays his typical character, a tough guy who has a way with the dames, she's

all sensual innocence and sexual sophistication, something that was decidedly different on the big screen. James Agee wrote that she had "cinema personality to burn . . . a javelinlike vitality, a born dancer's eloquence of movement, a fierce female shrewdness, and a special sweet-sourness. With these faculties, plus a stone-crushing self-confidence and a trombone voice, she manages to get across the toughest girl . . . Hollywood has dreamed of in a long, long while."

"Anybody got a match?" are Bacall's first words to Bogart in *To Have and Have Not.* He does, of course, since Bogart smoked his way through almost every movie he made. In fact, the whole ritual of lighting up and lingering over a cigarette was so stylized in movies of the '30s and '40s that smoking became a kind of foreplay for generations of audiences. And no couple generated as much heat by lighting up as Bogart and Bacall. "There are no strings tied around you," purrs Bacall through a haze of smoke, "not yet."

Certainly, Howard Hawks directed Bacall to her best advantage, not demanding too much and focusing on her stunning good looks. She plays a classy-looking blonde with a dubious background. Sure, she is a pickpocket, but she is no tramp. She just does what needs to be done. And from those baby-doll lips come the most suggestive lines.

"You know you don't have to act with me," Bacall tells Bogart. "You don't have to say anything, and you don't have to do anything. Oh, maybe just whistle. You know how to whistle, don't you, Steve? You just put your lips together and blow." These last two lines became their trademark, sealing their fate as a screen couple. Forever after, she would say the come-on lines and he would react—as only Bogie could—with astonishment and pleasure at his own good fortune in running into this dame.

In truth, *To Have and Have Not,* a thriller set in Martinique, was a second-rate *Casablanca* and looks like a cheap attempt to cash in on Bogie's fame. In fact, of Bogie and Bacall's four films together, none of them was more than adequate. But, as in all their collaborations, this movie is interesting for those moments when they are making eyes at each other.

Left and above:
From her very first movie, *To Have and Have Not,*
Bacall had "the look" that women envied and men admired.
From scene to scene, she could switch from seeming
innocence to crafty wisdom and, all the while,
remain unbelievably beautiful.

When she boldly kisses him, he asks: "Why'd you do that?" She shrugs those padded shoulders and says: "Been wondering if I'd like it." "What's the decision?" Bogart, baited and hooked, inquires. She coolly but knowingly replies: "It's even better when you help."

In real life, he did more than help. He divorced his third wife, Mayo Methot, and, on May 21, 1945, married Bacall. She was twenty, he forty-five. The press went berserk, and Bogie's reputation soared. In addition to being one of the biggest wartime actors, he had become a partner in one of Hollywood's most popular screen couples.

Their next film together was *The Big Sleep* (1946), a somewhat confusing adaptation of a Raymond Chandler novel. Accustomed to getting her own way, Bacall here is several notches up the social ladder from Slim, her character in *To Have and Have Not,* but she's basically the same type. Sophisticated and savvy, she

meets her match in Bogie, who lays down the rules when she complains about the way he talks to her. "I don't mind if you don't like my manners," he scowls. "I don't like them myself; they're pretty bad. I grieve over them long winter evenings. And I don't mind your ritzing me or drinking your lunch out of a bottle, but don't waste your time trying to cross-examine me."

In most of his movies, Bogart tended to treat women with both courtesy and contempt. He rarely smiled; his world-weary demeanor and ever-present cigarette suggested complete indifference to almost everything going on around him. But he could spot a phony at ten paces. He'd look a dame in the eye and say exactly what he thought. For example, in *The Big Sleep*, he uses his trademark deadpan delivery to describe Bacall's younger sister: "She tried to sit in my lap when I was standing up."

Women felt safe around Bogie, and with good cause. He could always handle himself—and anyone else. He'd outsmart everyone in the joint. Two steps ahead of the bad guys, he'd pursue them with dogged determination. His personal integrity was never in question. As critic Kenneth Tynan wrote: "We trusted him because he was a wary loner who belonged to nobody, (and) had personal honor. . . . "

Offscreen, Bacall changed Bogart's public image as a man adrift by himself. A loner herself, and a classy one at that, like Bogie, she was only alone by choice. They belonged together. She didn't smooth out his rough edges so much as she cushioned them a little, adding a touch of refinement and tenderness to his tough demeanor. Here, at last, was a woman who could keep up with him. On screen she matched his wicked wisecracks without blinking. In this classic Bogart-Bacall seduction scene from *The Big Sleep*, the double entendres turn triple somersaults:

Left, top and bottom:
"What's wrong with you?" Bogart asks Bacall in *The Big Sleep*, their second movie together. "Nothing you can't fix," she replies. Indeed. He's Philip Marlowe, the quintessential private eye, and she's a rich girl with family problems. No matter; with Marlowe on her case, she needn't worry about anything. He can fix what's broken and then some.
Opposite:
Although a kiss is just a kiss, it means a whole lot more when enacted by Bogart and Bacall. Or, more precisely, this wasn't acting; this was the real thing, and audiences knew it.

In *Dark Passage* Bacall says: "I was born lonely, I guess," which was typical of the kind of character both she and Bogie played, especially when they worked together.
Opposite:
Two loners in *Key Largo*.

BACALL: Speaking of horses, I like to play them myself. But I like to see them work out a little first. See if they're front-runners or come from behind. Find out what their hole card is. What makes them run.

BOGART: Find out mine?

BACALL: I think so. . . . I'd say you don't like to be rated. You like to get out in front, open up a lead, take a little breather in the back stretch, and then come home free.

BOGART: You don't like to be rated yourself.

BACALL: I haven't met anyone yet that could do it. Any suggestions?

BOGART: Well, I can't tell till I've seen you over a distance of ground. You've got a touch of class, but I don't know how far you can go.

BACALL: A lot depends on who's in the saddle.

Photographed in all the right restaurants and nightclubs, Bogart and Bacall were the idyllic romantic couple offscreen. Theirs was a fairy-tale romance—the stuff of more than one B movie. She helped obliterate

his reputation as a boozer and womanizer. She seemed to transform him into a happily married man, and made him a father for the first time. By the late 1940s, Bogart and Bacall were the most imitated couple in Hollywood. Men held their cigarettes like Bogie, and women tried to copy "Baby" Bacall's voice and "the look."

In 1947, Bogie formed his own production company, and the following year he appeared in one of his most memorable movies, *The Treasure of the Sierra Madre.* The same year, he made *Key Largo,* his last film with Bacall, helping re-establish her sagging career (which had suffered greatly when she lost Hawks as a director). She bought her contract back from Warner Brothers after being suspended a dozen times for refusing parts.

Bogart continued working, performing in some of his best movies, including *The African Queen, The Caine Mutiny, Sabrina,* and *The Barefoot Contessa.* In 1956 he had an operation for throat cancer, and he died the next year, at the age of fifty-seven. In his casket, Bacall placed a silver-plated whistle inscribed: "If you need me, whistle."

After Bogie died, Bacall returned to New York and a successful career on the Broadway stage, appearing in *Cactus Flower* (1966) and then winning two Tonys for her work in *Applause* (1970) and *Woman of the Year* (1981). She married actor Jason Robards and had another son with him. The couple divorced after eight years. Her 1978 autobiography, *By Myself,* was a national bestseller. She continues to work in films and as a spokeswoman in TV commercials.

In 1968 critic Pauline Kael praised Bogart by writing: "There isn't an actor in American films today with anything like his assurance, his magnetism or his style." More than thirty years after Bogart's death, his reputation as an actor and a screen presence continues to grow. He is often cited by critics as the first great antihero of American film. He once said that "the only thing you owe the public is a good performance," and he certainly made good on that debt. As David Shipman has written, Bogart "left a fine legacy, four or five films which are classics and a score which can be seen over and over. And are."

Legions of fans still follow Bogie's example and idolize his way with women. "The world is full of dames," says Woody Allen's imaginary Bogie. "All you gotta do is whistle."

Opposite and above:
In *Key Largo* Bogart and Bacall are held hostage during a tropical storm by tough guy Edward G. Robinson. Although Bogie and Bacall provided the film with a love interest, their relationship was secondary to the main plot, which revolved around Robinson. The stellar cast also included Lionel Barrymore and Claire Trevor, who won a Best Supporting Actress Oscar playing Robinson's boozy mistress.

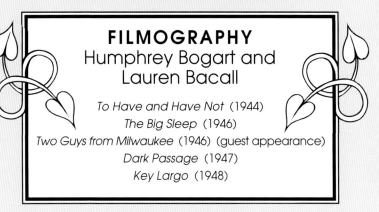

FILMOGRAPHY
Humphrey Bogart and Lauren Bacall

To Have and Have Not (1944)
The Big Sleep (1946)
Two Guys from Milwaukee (1946) (guest appearance)
Dark Passage (1947)
Key Largo (1948)

LEIGH & OLIVIER

"They presented the ultimate romantic vision.
A Heaven-made match. To see them together in life or on the screen was a heady experience.
They seemed to leave the real world and to exist an inch off the ground."

GARSON KANIN, *Together Again!* (1981)

Though they only made three movies together, Vivien Leigh and Laurence Olivier were one of the great screen couples of their time. Individually, they appeared in some of the most popular films ever made in Hollywood. She was the star of *Gone with the Wind, Waterloo Bridge,* and *A Streetcar Named Desire.* He made film history in such classics as *Wuthering Heights, Rebecca, Pride and Prejudice, Sleuth,* and *Marathon Man.* And the two actors appeared together on stage in numerous productions.

As a couple, they held special sway in Hollywood, New York, and London. They were respected and adored not only as celebrities who were in love with one another, but as the world's most talented, breathtakingly beautiful actors. Nothing could separate them, not even their marriages to other partners or their work on separate continents. After all, he was the most acclaimed actor of the twentieth century, and she was the screen's greatest beauty. They had to be together, and in true movie fantasy tradition they eventually were.

She was born in 1913 into a life of privilege in colonial India. At seventeen, she married Herbert Leigh Holman, and after the birth of a daughter she returned to her fledgling acting career. After playing a few small film parts, she became London's dramatic sensation on stage in *Mask of Virtue* in 1935. A few days after the play opened, producer Alexander Korda offered her a quarter of a million dollars for a five-year film contract.

Olivier, who was already an established actor, also saw her in the play. They met and fell in love. As the story goes, Leigh vowed that one day she would be Olivier's wife, even though they were then both married, with children.

Opposite and above:
"When the queen sends you home in disgrace, I'll come with you and be disgraced, too," Leigh promises Olivier in *Fire over England,* their first movie together, and we believe her. Surely, this is a love that will sacrifice all, and so it seemed in real life, too, as the couple struggled to obtain the necessary divorces from their respective spouses in order to be married.

Their first film together was *Fire over England* (1937). As a lady-in-waiting to Flora Robson's Queen Elizabeth, Leigh is wooed by Olivier, a stalwart for the

queen's cause. They were in love at the time, and it showed on screen. "We've a right to be happy," Leigh tells Olivier. "Everyone has a right to be happy." "Everyone, yes," replies Olivier. "That's why we can't be." (Offscreen, they were both struggling to obtain divorces.)

Leigh and Olivier then made *21 Days Together,* a dreadful British melodrama that wasn't released until two years after it was made, by which time they were both famous. Still, Olivier had not yet been granted his divorce, and Leigh decided to concentrate on her career. Although she was virtually unknown in Hollywood and had never even been to America, she pursued the most sought-after role in the history of movies: Scarlett O'Hara. In 1938, Leigh sailed to Hollywood, ostensibly to see Olivier.

Hollywood legend has it that producer David O. Selznick began shooting *Gone with the Wind* without having selected an actress to play Scarlett, and that he first laid eyes on Leigh while filming the burning of Atlanta. She was twenty-six years old when she won the coveted role and made it her own, though she later claimed: "I never liked Scarlett. I knew it was a marvelous part, but I never cared for her. I couldn't find anything of myself in her, except for one line. . . . It was the only thing in the character I could take hold of. It's in the scene after Frank's funeral, when she gets drunk and tells Rhett how glad she is her mother's dead and can't see her. 'She brought me up to be kind and thoughtful and ladylike, just like her, and I've been such a disappointment.' I liked her then, and perhaps in the end." (Even knowing this, can anyone imagine any other actress as Scarlett O'Hara?)

Leigh was miserable while filming *Gone with the Wind* because Olivier was three thousand miles away, appearing on Broadway. "She missed him so dreadfully that, one day, she got Selznick to let her come to New York to see a matinee of the play, *No Time for Comedy,*" Hollywood journalist Radie Harris has reported. "During intermission, she went back to see Larry, and they

Opposite:
In *21 Days Together* Leigh and Olivier play a modern couple who have only three weeks together before he must go on trial for murder. They make the most of every moment. Though the pair only worked together on three films, in every one of them, their love was dangerous or forbidden or both. Ironically, this was a reflection of their real-life romance.

In *That Hamilton Woman,* Leigh and Olivier reenacted the illicit love affair between Lady Hamilton and Lord Nelson, and they were never more well cast. "Oh my darling, why do we always meet just to say goodbye," she sobs as he leaves to fight yet another battle. Unfortunately, this was their last film together, although they frequently costarred on stage. Why Hollywood didn't hire them as a screen couple remains a mystery.

clasped and clung to each other so that you'd think it was the farewell scene to *Romeo and Juliet.*"

Their respective divorces finally came through, and they eloped in 1940. Director-writer Garson Kanin, who witnessed their marriage vows, claimed they fought all the way to the justice of the peace. Leigh and Olivier were, in fact, known for their screaming battles and for making scenes in the company of friends. Theirs was a "romance of classic proportions," Douglas Fairbanks, Jr., once said.

There was a certain irony to their being a couple, says writer Sewell Stokes: "He was considered an excellent actor who might have improved his position in the theater had he not sold himself to the movies. She was adored by film fans and politely told by the critics when she appeared on the stage that she was lovely to look at." In the end, both would reverse critical opinion and win praise for their work in film and on the stage.

They made *That Hamilton Woman* in 1941. He played Lord Nelson, and she was his mistress, Lady Hamilton. During a clandestine meeting, they talk about their love for each other, which was symbolic of the time Leigh and Olivier had spent together before being married:

OLIVIER: You shouldn't have come. People will see you; they'll talk.
LEIGH: Oh, let them talk. I don't care. Do you? Are you sorry?
OLIVIER: I'm only sorry for all the wasted years I've been without you. For all the years I shall have to be without you.
LEIGH: You'll come back, won't you?
OLIVIER: I wonder if I shall. I feel that I should not. You are married, and I am married. In the magic and music of the ballroom, these things become rather blurred. But they stand out very clearly in the dawn. Your life is here; my life is there. We must obey the creed and codes that we've sworn our lives to. I know that I must not come back, and I know that nothing in this world can keep me away.

When the war broke out, the Oliviers did their patriotic duty. He joined the Royal Air Force, and she, though always frail, worked hard for the war effort. In 1944 she collapsed on stage, suffered a miscarriage, and started showing signs of an emotional illness that would plague her for the rest of her life. Diagnosed with tuberculosis, she refused to take care of herself. Some critics claimed that many of her problems were caused by her constantly being compared to her husband and found wanting. She was disappointed about not being cast more often with Olivier. "I confess I should dearly liked to have played with my husband in the films of *Wuthering Heights* and *Rebecca*," she told Garson Kanin. "They gave me abundant tests for the heroine in the latter film in Hollywood, then came to the conclusion that I looked 'foxy.' An epithet with which I quite wildly disagree." Nonetheless, her confidence slipped. She went into and out of institutions and sanatoriums.

Olivier once explained the difficulties of their acting and living together: "It is unfortunate that Vivien's and my conversations, which should be normal conversations, are all too frequently conferences about some business problem or some theater problem."

In 1945, Olivier began his most productive period. He produced, directed, and starred in *Henry V*, which won him a special Oscar. Three years later, he matched his success with *Hamlet*, which won Oscars for both Best Actor and Best Film. In 1947, when Olivier was only forty years old, he was knighted, becoming the youngest theater person to receive that honor. The knighthood only increased the image of the Oliviers as a great romantic couple. "They really were the King and Queen of the theater," said Sir John Gielgud.

Leigh and Olivier appeared together on stage in a number of plays, *School for Scandal, Macbeth,* and *Antony and Cleopatra*, to name only a few. His reputation as an actor, director, and producer soared, and she struggled to keep up with him. In 1951 she took on the role of Blanche DuBois in *A Streetcar Named Desire* (after Olivia de Havilland had turned it down) and won her second Oscar. Tennessee Williams paid Leigh the highest possible tribute, telling *Life* that she had brought to the part everything he had intended and much that he had never dreamed of.

Leigh's portrayal of Blanche exposed her own despondency and fragility, which were becoming more and more of a burden. She experienced wild mood swings, and Olivier felt pressured to compensate for her erratic behavior. She would often throw tantrums, breaking windows and otherwise behaving badly. She underwent shock treatment. They toured together in *Titus Andronicus,* and, although she was at her worst, she stayed with the production. Under constant public scrutiny their marriage began to unravel.

Then Olivier starred in the play *The Entertainer,* which had been written expressly for him by John Osborne. Leigh was considered too beautiful to appear as his wife, and too old to play his daughter. During production, Olivier fell in love with his young costar, Joan Plowright. According to Olivier's friend Virginia Fairweather, he was "racked with worry and guilt and horror at the unavoidable scandal that would ensue if there should be a divorce between him and Vivien. Like any man labelled 'the guilty party' he was conscience-stricken at the idea of ending a marriage that had meant so much even though it had now gone sour. . . . He didn't wish to hurt Vivien; at the same time he had terrible remorse about the harm publicity might do to Joan. His previous marriage had been annulled when he was relatively unknown, but this time, inevitably, it would make the headlines, almost like royalty."

The great romance of this golden couple had burned itself out, and their divorce set off an avalanche of unwelcomed publicity. Leigh appeared in two more films, *The Roman Spring of Mrs. Stone* and *Ship of Fools*. It was said that she kept Olivier's picture and love letters by her bed. She died of tuberculosis in 1967, at the age of fifty-three. "Poor, dear Vivien," Olivier reportedly said when told of her death.

Olivier's career spanned several more decades. Nominated for a total of twelve Oscars as an actor, a producer, and a director, he won twice and also garnered two special Oscars. In 1970 he was made a life peer, which allowed him to sit in the House of Lords. (He is the only actor ever to have been granted such an honor). When asked how he would prefer to be addressed, Olivier suggested: "How about Lord Larry?"

In all, he appeared in more than 120 stage roles, 60 films, and 15 television productions. He directed and produced thirty-eight plays, and directed six films and six plays for television. In 1978 he received his second special Oscar, for "the full body of his work, the unique achievement of his entire career and his lifetime of contribution to the art of film." Lord Olivier died of cancer in 1989, at the age of eighty-two.

Looking back, it seems obvious that Leigh and Olivier were the genuine article; they made real what others merely played at. Their romance was an event of worldwide interest. When they married in 1940, newspapers put them in the select company of such great lovers as Romeo and Juliet and the Duke and Duchess of Windsor. The Oliviers' relationship was called "the most idyllic of modern off-stage romances." For nearly twenty years, they were the most perfect couple of their time: movie stars, theatrical royalty, patriots, great and stormy lovers, and devoted husband and wife. That the dream eventually faded did not detract from its power. Leigh and Olivier are as real to us today as Scarlett O'Hara and Heathcliff; such larger-than-life characters, like the actors who portrayed them, live on forever.

FILMOGRAPHY
Vivien Leigh and Laurence Olivier

Fire over England (1937)
21 Days Together (1937)
That Hamilton Woman (1941)

TAYLOR & BURTON

"The purest celebrities we have in show business . . .
are Mr. and Mrs. Burton. . . .
They have never made an especially good movie and probably never will."

WILFRID SHEED, *Esquire* (October 1968)

Hounded by gossip columnists, journalists, and photographers from both sides of the Atlantic, Elizabeth Taylor and Richard Burton were among the foremost celebrities of the '60s and early '70s. Their every move was seized on by the press: the jewelry he bought her, the yachts they sailed on, the endless fights and reconciliations. They tried to build a private life together that combined love, work, marriage, and children, but their notorious marriage was constantly prey to public opinion. The personification of Hollywood glamour, their romance was as much about fantasy as were their films.

While living in the spotlight, they made eleven movies, many of them mediocre at best, unwatchable at worst. In fact, their styles and talents were so divergent that, if they hadn't been a couple, it's doubtful they ever would have been cast together. Thus, their movies suffered, and perhaps the strain of so many failed efforts helped destroy their marriage.

The Burtons, and the publicity they generated, were a throwback to the Hollywood of the '40s; the '60s equivalent of Bogart and Bacall or Garbo and Gilbert. They were known throughout the world simply as Liz and Dick. "The Burtons at love or war (were) about the last of their kind," said the *New York Times Magazine*.

Perhaps the greatest American beauty of her day, Taylor was only ten years old when both Universal and MGM were vying for her. She made her acting debut in

Opposite:
"But I will never be free of you," Burton says to Taylor in *Cleopatra*, their first and most spectacular movie together. The sentiment echoed their sensational and stormy relationship, which was to last for the next decade. Theirs was a romance that both titillated audiences and inspired journalists around the world.

There's One Born Every Minute (1942) and then appeared in two *Lassie* movies in 1943 and 1946. Her starring role in *National Velvet* (1944) brought rave reviews. "The performance of Elizabeth Taylor is a lovely conception," stated the *New York World-Telegram*, "a burning eagerness tempered with sweet, fragile charm." She held great promise, although the *World-Telegram* aptly noted that, "for quite some time to come, she is likely to stir up more fuss off screen than on."

Taylor's beauty was so extraordinary that she seemed to skip the awkward adolescent stage, transformed from beautiful little girl to enchanting young woman. Though she played a few teenage roles, it really seemed as though she went straight from child parts to romantic leads in such movies as *Father of the Bride*. At the age of seventeen she was being courted by Howard Hughes. The same year, she wed hotelier Nick Hilton, soon divorcing him and marrying actor Michael Wilding and then showman Mike Todd. When Todd died in a plane crash only a year after their wedding, Taylor snagged Eddie Fisher (Todd's best man) from Debbie Reynolds and gained a reputation as a home wrecker. It wasn't until Taylor suffered a rare and nearly fatal form of pneumonia that her fans forgave her indiscretion. Some say that public sympathy about her health problems helped earn her an Academy Award for *Butterfield 8* in 1960.

The Oscar made her more valuable on the set of *Cleopatra*, the movie that would change everything for Taylor and Burton and would almost bankrupt 20th Century-Fox in the process. *Cleopatra* began with a million-dollar budget, but was so beset with problems it ended up costing more than $40 million. Rouben Mamoulian, the original director, began shooting with

Taylor in the title role, Peter Finch as Caesar (Laurence Olivier had rejected the part), and Stephen Boyd as Antony. Production was halted for several months when Taylor fell ill. Mamoulian resigned with only about ten minutes of film (costing over $6 million) in the can, and he was replaced by Joseph L. Mankiewicz. Then, Taylor was quoted as saying: "It will be fun to be the first Jewish Queen of Egypt," and Egyptian authorities revoked permission for Fox to shoot key scenes in that country. Therefore, expensive sets had to be built. The production was so delayed that both Finch and Boyd had to bow out due to previous commitments; they were replaced by Rex Harrison and Richard Burton.

Seven years Taylor's senior, Burton made his reputation on the stage. Born in South Wales and the youngest of thirteen children, he worked his way to the London stage, where he became known primarily for his interpretations of Shakespearean roles. He went to Hollywood in 1952 to star opposite Olivia de Havilland in *My Cousin Rachel*. "Burton, lean and handsome, is the perfect hero for Miss Daphne du Maurier's tale," said the *New York Times*. "His outbursts of ecstasy and torment are in the grand romantic style." Critics compared him to grand old actors such as John Barrymore and Edmund Kean. Until the making of *Cleopatra*, Burton had been "considered the heir to Olivier as England's greatest actor. In fact, Olivier sent a wire to Burton on the set of *Cleopatra* stating: 'Make up your mind, dear heart. Do you want to be a great actor or a household word?' Burton's reply: 'Both.'"

His affair with Taylor certainly made him a household word. Their increasingly torrid relationship during the filming of *Cleopatra* was touted around the world. Torn between husband Eddie Fisher and lover Burton, Taylor reportedly attempted suicide.

On the set, all pretense of domestic calm evaporated when Eddie Fisher and Sybil Williams Burton left Rome, generating even more adverse publicity. The world waited for *Cleopatra* to be released, hoping to see stormy love scenes and romantic entanglements worthy of such press.

The film finally opened in New York on June 12, 1963, amid a flurry of expectation. In the *New York Herald-Tribune* Judith Crist summed up the general reaction to the film, calling it "at best a major disappointment, at worst an extravagant exercise in tedium." The film did not fare well with the fans either. Nominated for nine Academy Awards, it only won four: Cinematography, Art Direction, Costumes, and Special Visual Effects. When the television rights to the film were sold in 1966, *Cleopatra* was still $10 million in the red. "I found it vulgar," Taylor said of the movie. "Yes, I suppose I should be grateful about having made the picture, for obvious reasons."

However, *Cleopatra* was a failure on such a grand scale that the public clamored for more of the Burtons. Not only larger than life, they were larger than 20th Century-Fox, and perhaps their colossal failure made them seem more human. God and goddess with human hearts, they would survive in spite of the critics and the bad showing at the box office. Sometimes love does conquer all in real life as well as on the big screen.

Several producers were quick to cash in on the Burtons' fame. They starred together in a seemingly

Above and opposite:
In *The V.I.P.s* Taylor and Burton were among the rich and beautiful, playing to type in this drama set in an airport. He was relatively unknown to Hollywood before his romance with Taylor catapulted him to fame and fortune and, at the same time, somewhat diminished his status as a serious actor.

From the very beginning of their relationship, both personal and professional, Taylor and Burton
were a photographer's dream and a publicist's nightmare. Two immensely attractive people, obviously in love,
they photographed well, as is evident in these two stills from *The V.I.P.s*, but they had little privacy
from the press. From the first hints of their tempestuous, illicit relationship to their
much-publicized break-ups and reconciliations, the Burtons were always front-page news.

endless stream of overly sentimental films. Several of them, such as *The V.I.P.s* and *The Sandpiper*, were written expressly for the couple. In *The Sandpiper* Taylor tells Burton: "Men have been staring at me and rubbing up against me ever since I was twelve years old. They've been waiting for me to stumble so that they can close in. Sometimes, I get the suffocating feeling that they will. And I see myself, perhaps tomorrow, perhaps next year, being handed from man to man as if I were an amusement from men who've only really had me, never really loved me."

Though *The Sandpiper* is far from a great movie, it still grossed more than $7 million in 1965, proving that the couple didn't have to make good movies; they could carry a film on their celebrity alone.

Taylor once tried to explain their appeal to the public: "Maybe Richard and I are sex symbols together because we suggest love. At first, illicit love. And it seems curious that our society today finds illicit love

Opposite:
Advertisements for *The Sandpiper* declared: "Taylor and Burton's real-life passion sparks this tale of forbidden love," thus further obscuring the line between their personal and professional life. Here Burton plays an uptight, married, and religious man while she's a free spirit who lives in a million-dollar beach house and supports herself selling watercolors.

Above:
Certainly, the crowning artistic achievement for Taylor and Burton was *Who's Afraid of Virginia Woolf?*, nominated for twelve Oscars and winning for Best Actress (Taylor), Best Supporting Actress (Sandy Dennis), Cinematography, Art Direction, and Costume Design, although Burton lost his Best Actor nomination to Paul Scofield (*A Man for All Seasons*). The film also marked the directorial debut and first Oscar nomination of Mike Nichols.
Right: (top and bottom)
In a harrowing indictment of marriage, Burton and Taylor relentlessly insult and torture each other in this film, inventing sadistic games wherein they reenact their most neurotic passions. In the end, the characters conclude no one knows the difference between truth and illusion. "True," says Burton, "but we must carry on anyway."

more attractive than married love. Our love is married now, but there is still a suggestion, I suppose, of rampant sex on the wild."

To the public, they became more important than their art, and they seemed to know no shame. In March 1965 Burton wrote an article for *Vogue* describing his first impression of Taylor: "Her breasts were apocalyptic, they would topple empires down before they withered. Indeed, her body was a miracle of construction and the work of an engineer of genius. It needed nothing except itself. It was true art, I thought, executed in terms of itself." (*Vogue* inserted a disclaimer at the start of the article, explaining that Burton "dislikes any editing, cannot bear to have his work touched.")

Above:
The couple fared slightly better when they made a stab at
Shakespeare's classic play *The Taming of the Shrew,* which was
directed with flair by Franco Zeffirelli. Burton was certainly
more in his element as Petruchio, and Taylor delivered
the goods as the man-hating Kate.

Right, top and bottom:
An uninspired adaptation of a Graham Greene novel, *The
Comedians* concerned political intrigue in Haiti under
Papa Doc Duvalier. Burton and Taylor get involved in a
situation they can't quite understand, and neither can the
audience. The film marked the beginning of a rapid decline in
Burton and Taylor's popularity as a screen couple.
Although they would make four more movies together, none
of them would come close to recapturing their former
fame or success.

Less objective writers saw the couple quite dif-
ferently. In 1968 *Esquire* claimed: "Whether husbands
and wives should work together is a question. . . . But
surely couples shouldn't act together when the differential in talent is as great as this. Mr. Burton may be
very good . . . but he is not good enough, either in
acting or in acting tactics, to carry a subaverage film

actress like Miss Taylor through whole movies; they simply fall down on top of each other."

Perhaps the only noteworthy film the Burtons ever made together was *Who's Afraid of Virginia Woolf?*

Released in the United States in 1973, *Under Milk Wood,* an attempt to bring Dylan Thomas's lyric verse radio play to the screen, was such a dismal artistic and critical failure that it virtually ended their partnership in theatrical films. They were relegated to television, appearing regularly on late-night talk shows.

Though their big-screen work as a couple ceased, their celebrity lived on. They starred together in *Divorce His—Divorce Hers,* an ABC television movie that *Variety* claimed only proved "Liz and Dick are the corniest act in show business. . . . Miss Taylor wallowed in suds to a point where the many closeups between her ample bazooms failed even in distracting from the nonsense. Burton was wooden-legged and wooden-lipped, and seemed to grow stiffer as the two-night fiasco crept on its petty pace." After *Divorce His—Divorce Hers,* Burton would tell an interviewer: "We cannot just go on playing ourselves."

On July 3, 1973, Taylor announced that she and Burton were separating. In a press release she wrote:

"Maybe we have loved each other too much—not that I ever believed such a thing was possible—but we have been in each other's pockets constantly, never being apart except for matters of life or death, and I believe with all my heart that this separation will ultimately bring us back to where we should be—and that is: together!"

They divorced in the early 1970s, then reconciled and separated several more times amid much publicity. They remarried in 1975 and then divorced again the following year. Each remarried other partners and continued to work. Burton was nominated six times for an Oscar but never won. He died in 1984, at the age of fifty-nine, of a cerebral hemorrhage.

Beset by addictions, Taylor has become more well known for her weight swings, numerous marriages, hospitalizations, and charity work for AIDS than for her acting. Today, she works primarily in television and made-for-cable movies. She remains one of the most visible celebrities in the world. In the end, perhaps, the overexposed love affair between the American sex symbol and the dashing Welsh actor might have played better as a movie plot than it did in real life.

Opposite:
Taylor and Burton in a scene from
The Comedians, **with costar James Earl Jones.**

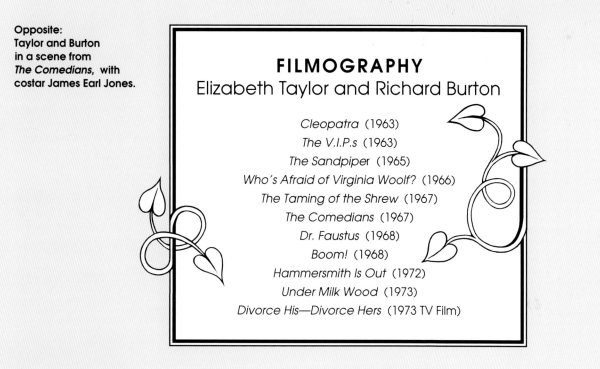

FILMOGRAPHY
Elizabeth Taylor and Richard Burton

Cleopatra (1963)

The V.I.P.s (1963)

The Sandpiper (1965)

Who's Afraid of Virginia Woolf? (1966)

The Taming of the Shrew (1967)

The Comedians (1967)

Dr. Faustus (1968)

Boom! (1968)

Hammersmith Is Out (1972)

Under Milk Wood (1973)

Divorce His—Divorce Hers (1973 TV Film)

NEWMAN & WOODWARD

"Theirs is the most famous marriage in filmdom and perhaps in all of America. . . ."

LARRY ROTHER, The *New York Times* (November 18, 1990)

Paul Newman and Joanne Woodward are, in some ways, the exact opposite of Elizabeth Taylor and Richard Burton. The Newmans live private lives, shunning the superstardom that ultimately destroyed the marriage of the Burtons.

Newman and Woodward don't reside in Hollywood or promote themselves on talk shows, and they're rarely mentioned in gossip columns or photographed in public. They only give interviews when absolutely necessary, to publicize a new movie or speak out for an important cause. Yet, even without the glitz and glamour, Newman and Woodward are considered one of the most legendary couples in movie history.

Their marriage has endured for more than thirty years, during which time they have starred together in ten films, and he has directed her in four more. Active politically, they both campaign for liberal causes and candidates. They founded a drug treatment center in Los Angeles when Newman's son from his first marriage died of an overdose of alcohol and drugs. Newman has served as a United States delegate to the United Nations conference on disarmament. They each have many other interests: he races cars; she's active in the arts and recently completed her college education. Newman's line of food products—salad dressing, popcorn, lemonade—grosses more than $30 million a year.

Opposite:
A memorable scene from *WUSA*, one of the lesser-known movies starring Paul Newman and Joanne Woodward. Here, Newman plays a disc jockey who becomes disillusioned by the political policies of a New Orleans radio station, WUSA. Though the movie had its flaws, certainly the love scenes were believable.

He donates the profits to various charities. They live a relatively quiet life in Connecticut, where they have raised three daughters.

Both Newman and Woodward came to New York in the early 1950s in order to break into acting. They met in their agent's office in the summer of 1953. "I had been making the rounds," Woodward remembers, "and I was hot, sweaty and my hair was all stringy around my neck. He (the agent, Maynard Morris) brought out a pretty-looking young man in a seersucker suit, all pretty like an Arrow Collar ad, and said, 'This is Paul Newman,' and I hated him on sight, but he was so funny and pretty and neat." Though Newman was married at the time, they became friends. They had much in common. Both worked extensively in television, especially in live productions of various dramas. Then, they worked together in the stage production of *Picnic*.

Newman was cast in the leading role, and Woodward understudied two of the female parts. The hit play launched his career. He was given a contract by Warner Brothers, and soon appeared in several movies, including *Somebody Up There Likes Me,* which made him one of Hollywood's hottest properties in 1956. Two years later, he starred in *The Left-Handed Gun, The Long, Hot Summer,* and *Cat on a Hot Tin Roof,* for which he received an Oscar nomination.

Woodward's career skyrocketed at about the same time. She was a relative unknown in 1957 when she was cast as the lead in *The Three Faces of Eve.* The part had originally been assigned to Judy Garland, and then Susan Hayward, Doris Day, Jennifer Jones, and June Allyson were considered. When none of these actresses were available, Woodward won the role by

default—one of those coincidences that make movie magic. Her portrayal of a disturbed woman with three distinct personalities was nothing short of miraculous. The movie got mixed reviews, but Woodward was a sensation. The *New York Times* said that she played the role "with superlative flexibility and emotional power." Rated the top female find of the year in the *Film Daily* poll, she won the Oscar for Best Actress in 1957, creating a scandal when she wore to the ceremonies a dress she had made herself. "Joanne Woodward is setting the cause of Hollywood glamour back by twenty years by making her own clothes," griped Joan Crawford. But it was a typical Woodward gesture, and the fans loved her for it.

Five years after Woodward and Newman met, he divorced his first wife. He married Woodward in late January 1958. The same year, they made their first film together, *The Long, Hot Summer*. Based on short stories by William Faulkner, the film established character types—the hustler and the well-bred southern lady—that each would play again and again. He was "as mean and keen as a cackle-eyed scythe," and she played

"her part with a fire and grace not often seen in a movie queen," proclaimed *Time* on March 29, 1958.

At the beginning of the movie, they seem exact opposites. She's all repressed desires, and he swaggers through town radiating sexuality. "I have a feeling I rile you," he tells her. She seethes at his advances, cutting him off before he can make his move. "Miss Clara, you slam the door in a man's face before he even knocks on it," he says with a mocking grin. He then tries a more direct approach with her: "I can see you don't like me, but you're going to have me. . . . I'll tell you one thing, you're going to wake up smiling in the morning."

She reacts instantly, revealing the strength and self-confidence hidden deep within her character.

"You got some foolish ideas about me, Mr. Quick," she tells him. "I'm no trembling little rabbit full of smoldering unsatisfied desires. . . . I'm a woman, full grown, very smart and not at all bad to look at. . . . And I expect to live at the top of my head without help from you. . . . You are barking up the wrong girl."

By the end of the film, it is Newman who has changed: "You're a hard-headed, soft-hearted woman, Miss Clara, and I like you a lot. You couldn't tame me but you taught me."

He decides to leave town, give up the dream of fitting into Woodward's world. Now, she can come to him. She repeats the speech he had previously spoken to her: "So you run and keep on running, and you buy

yourself a bus ticket, and you disappear. And you change your name, and you dye your hair, and maybe, just maybe, you might be safe from me." They've come full circle.

The Long, Hot Summer is one of the most satisfying movies Newman and Woodward have made together because they play characters so well suited to their own personalities. Also, the film is the kind of complex, layered drama that suits them best as actors. They made their worst movies when they strayed into other genres, attempting light comedy in such films as *Rally 'Round the Flag, Boys!* A suburban spoof, it was meant for a couple such as Cary Grant and Irene Dunne, and the Newmans lacked the touch to make the material work. "When I wasn't playing small, I was making faces," Woodward once said about the movie. "I loathed myself in it."

Paris Blues (1961) was another attempt to mix genres. Jazzmen Newman and Sidney Poitier romance Woodward and Diahann Carroll, who play two Americans on vacation. In explaining the problem with the film, author James Parrish wrote: "In its sociological aim, *Paris Blues* falls loosely somewhere between the film *The Defiant Ones* (1958) and the Broadway musical *No Strings* (1962)."

Also set in Paris, the Newmans' next film, *A New Kind of Love*, trapped them in a vehicle more suited to a couple such as Tony Curtis and Janet Leigh. In this mistaken-identity story, businesswoman Woodward disguises herself as a blonde streetwalker and is picked up by Newman, who, of course, doesn't recognize her as the tough cookie he met on the plane to Paris. Wrote Judith Crist in the *New York Herald-Tribune:* "These two usually distinguished performers are entitled to a fling—but Doris Day and Rock Hudson they're not—and shouldn't aspire to be." The *Washington Post* noted: "Even were the material witty, I have the sad feeling the Newmans wouldn't be at home in it." Obviously, screen comedy didn't suit this husband-wife team.

Left, top and bottom:
Based on the popular John O'Hara novel, *From the Terrace*
was the third movie starring Newman and Woodward.
Here, Newman is a young war veteran who returns home and
marries socially prominent but pampered Woodward.
In describing her new husband to a friend, Woodward says
he's a "delicious man and all man from the top of
his head to the tip of his toes."

As Newman builds a financial empire in *From the Terrace*, Woodward begins to feel abandoned and rejected. Though she never looked more gorgeous or sophisticated, Woodward plays a woman who is both selfish and vain. She has an affair with an old beau, but Newman is comforted by Ina Balin, the daughter of one of his business associates. Ultimately, the movie was panned by critics for being little more than a high-class soap opera. Yet, *From the Terrace* remains a tribute to the acting talents of both Newman and Woodward, who almost make it work as an entertaining (if somewhat superficial) romantic drama.

Once the couple began their family, Woodward placed her children and husband before her career. For most of the 1960s, she stayed home to raise their daughters. She made only ten films during this decade, none of them particularly noteworthy except for the insightful *Rachel, Rachel* (which Newman directed).

During the same period, Paul Newman made twenty films, several of them among his most popular and best work, including *The Hustler*, *Hud*, *Cool Hand Luke*, and *Butch Cassidy and the Sundance Kid*. These were Newman's glory years. "A winning combination of an athletic physique, classic handsome features, expres-

sive blue eyes, an intelligent grasp of roles, and a captivating sense of humor, established Newman in the '60s as a favorite star among filmgoers and critics alike," writes film historian Ephraim Katz.

At the height of his popularity, Newman also gave his infamous interview to *Playboy.* When asked to speak about infidelity, he said: "Why should I go out for hamburger when I have steak at home?" The remark still infuriates Woodward. "That could've ended our relationship," she told Connie Chung in a recent TV interview. "What a chauvinist statement! I am not a piece of meat. . . . Every time that quote pops up, I want to kill." On the same show, Newman admitted to Chung that he rued the day he made the remark, but he had to concede that "it was a rather accurate assessment."

In the '70s Newman cofounded the production company First Artists along with Barbra Streisand, Sidney Poitier, and Steve McQueen. This gave Newman more control over his work. In addition to *Rachel, Rachel* he produced and directed many movies, including three others starring Woodward: *The Effect of Gamma Rays on Man-in-the-Moon Marigolds, The Shadow Box,* and *The Glass Menagerie.* She continued to work in television, winning an Emmy in 1978 for her performance in the TV movie *See How She Runs.*

In 1984 Newman wrote and directed *Harry and Son,* which is about the troubled relationship between a father and son. It touches on many personal issues, and critics claim it was based, at least partly, on Newman's relationship with his son, Scott, who had died in the late 1970s. Woodward has a small part in the film which, she has admitted, was "sort of made up. . . . I was going on location so I said, 'If I'm going on location, you should write a part for me.'"

Though Newman has been nominated for an Academy Award many times, he didn't receive one until 1985, when he was honored for lifetime achievement. In his acceptance speech he reminded the Academy not to write him off as a contender. The following year he won the Oscar for Best Actor for *The Color of Money.*

In most of their later films, the couple is far better than their material, and, perhaps for this reason, their

Opposite, top and bottom:
In their eighth movie together, *The Drowning Pool,*
Joanne Woodward plays a rich southern lady
who hires Paul Newman, her ex-lover, to find out who is
sending her blackmail letters.

Above:
Newman directed, coproduced, and worked on the
script of *Harry and Son,* a family drama about the conflicts
between an aging blue-collar worker and his
free-spirited son, played by Robby Benson.
Woodward played Newman's friend and neighbor.

collaborations have been few and far between. But in 1990, they appeared in *Mr. & Mrs. Bridge,* a film about a staid marriage that reverberates with deep undercurrents; it has been praised as their best collaborative work. In the *New York Times* Vincent Canby wrote: "Newman and Woodward give what are possibly the

image of perfection: "It's certainly an exciting marriage. But I don't know that it's the Rock of Gibraltar or without deep holes and rainbarrels and all that stuff. I mean, it's a very complicated thing—two people together for as long as we've been together." What makes it work, he said, is "respect, I think, ultimately."

In the same interview, Woodward added: "We make each other laugh. That's really the best thing of all."

Woodward plays the subservient wife of Newman in *Mr. & Mrs. Bridge*, a movie based on two novels by Evan S. Connell. Set in Kansas City in the years between the two World Wars, the film tracks the day-to-day lives of a straight-laced middle-class couple and their three children. Some critics faulted the film for its rather slow pace; others declared it a subtle masterpiece. In either case, the movie certainly showcases the extraordinary acting talents of Woodward and Newman, who imbue this couple with a depth of feeling that is totally convincing.

best performances of their careers as the title roles, two people who might have been born with their clothes on, wearing, of course, the right shoes and socks. The film looks at the placid surface of this upper-middle-class marriage and sees the depths beneath that, most of the time, Mr. and Mrs. Bridge avoid thinking about."

The film is a fitting vehicle for this couple who have managed, somehow, to build a reasonably normal life outside the Hollywood maelstrom, a feat few others have even come close to accomplishing. If any two movie stars married to one another have ever been seen as a perfect couple, it is the Newmans. Yet, in a rare moment, Newman was honest enough to dispel the

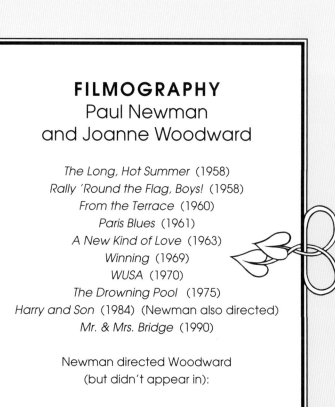

FILMOGRAPHY
Paul Newman
and Joanne Woodward

The Long, Hot Summer (1958)
Rally 'Round the Flag, Boys! (1958)
From the Terrace (1960)
Paris Blues (1961)
A New Kind of Love (1963)
Winning (1969)
WUSA (1970)
The Drowning Pool (1975)
Harry and Son (1984) (Newman also directed)
Mr. & Mrs. Bridge (1990)

Newman directed Woodward
(but didn't appear in):

Rachel, Rachel (1968)
The Effect of Gamma Rays on Man-in-the-Moon Marigolds (1972)
The Shadow Box (1980 TV Film)
The Glass Menagerie (1987)

PART THREE

lovers on and offscreen

TRACY & HEPBURN

"We were the perfect male/female of that era—American style.
The woman coming into her own and the man trying to blockade her . . .
get her but blockade her."

KATHARINE HEPBURN

Katharine Hepburn strode into Hollywood wearing her signature slacks and refusing to participate in the rigmarole of publicity. From the very beginning she would not give interviews or participate in press conferences. She didn't mingle with the Hollywood crowd, shunned autograph seekers, and even refused to frequent restaurants. Dignified and arrogant, she set her own style, and reporters soon discovered that her private life was strictly private. In 1935 a *Photoplay* headline read: "Is Hepburn Killing Her Own Career?"

More than fifty years later, she explained her reasoning in a rare television interview: "I thought, if I'm a success, it's one thing, but if I'm a flop and I've just had all that publicity, it will wreck my life. . . . Why should they advertise something that the public hasn't said, 'Oh, we rather like her, you know'—or the critics. Nobody had said anything. I didn't want to be pre-sold." She needn't have worried, for as George Cukor once remarked: "It can frankly be said that Hepburn has not grown up to Hollywood. Hollywood has grown up to her."

Hepburn started acting in college and made her professional stage debut in 1928, the same year she married Philadelphia socialite broker Ludlow Ogden

Opposite:
**Spencer Tracy and Katharine Hepburn are among a handful of superstars whose appeal has not diminished over the years. More than two decades after his death, he remains one of the most admired actors of all time.
And she is still one of the most talented and beautiful women to grace the big screen. Art Buchwald once called her prominent cheekbones, "the greatest calcium deposits since the White Cliffs of Dover."**

Smith (they divorced in 1934). She became a Broadway star in 1932 and signed with RKO when Cukor demanded her for *A Bill of Divorcement* with John Barrymore. The film was a hit, and by her third film, *Morning Glory,* she had copped an Oscar.

A star from the moment she stepped off the train in Los Angeles, Hepburn had a voice that Tallulah Bankhead described as sounding like nickels dropping into a slot. About her own voice Hepburn has said: "I talk fast and I talk loud, but I have wonderful thoughts going on in my head." As a child, she had fantasized about being a Hollywood star, but, like everything else about her, her dreams were out of the ordinary: "I wanted to be William S. Hart, Tom Mix, anyone like that. I wanted to ride a horse."

Hepburn's stellar career, though, was not all a garden of calla lilies in bloom. She was often fired from jobs, and she flopped on stage rather frequently. In 1934, her appearance on Broadway in *The Lake* provoked the acerbic writer Dorothy Parker to comment: "Hepburn ran the gamut of emotions from A to B."

Hepburn returned to Hollywood, making several more movies, including *Bringing Up Baby* with Cary Grant, in which she displayed a talent for screwball comedy. But her films didn't always do well at the box office. When RKO tried to force her to appear in *Mother Carey's Chickens,* she bought back her contract and cast around for a job.

Even when Hepburn was labeled box-office poison, she never allowed her setbacks to stop her: "When I was down in the gutter and couldn't get a job, I thought, well, that's not going to beat me." And it didn't. She came back again and again. "The secret

Lardner, Jr., and Michael Kanin). She wanted to work with director George Stevens, who'd been her director on several RKO projects. She wanted a long-term contract with the standard superstar perks. And she wanted Spencer Tracy.

"I admired him," she has said of Tracy. "He just had an amazing direction in his funny, old eyes. He just was sensitive. . . . He was really a brilliant actor . . . very vulnerable."

She got everything she demanded from MGM, including Tracy. The story of their first meeting has assumed the fine patina of Hollywood legend. When introduced by producer Joseph L. Mankiewicz, Hepburn gave Tracy the once-over. "You're rather *short*, aren't you?" commented Hepburn. "Don't worry, honey," said Mankiewicz, "he'll cut you down to size."

Tracy was, of course, a major star when he first met Hepburn in 1941. He was, and perhaps still is, considered one of the greatest screen actors of all time. "Tracy was one of the few actors whose career went only in an upward curve," writes David Shipman. "Not all his films were hits, but his career had no reversals, and he went from being a solid, reliable young actor to

Above and right:
When political commentator Hepburn suggests abolishing baseball for the duration of World War II, sports writer Tracy writes a scathing column denouncing her in *Woman of the Year*, their first film together.
His opinion of her changes after they meet privately in her office. Soon, they're making wedding plans.
The movie makes the case that mutual respect and intelligent conversation can be romantic and that a woman can be as smart as a man, or even smarter, and still be desirable.

of life is how you survive failure," Hepburn has remarked, half joking.

She avenged her theater critics when she asked Philip Barry, the author of the show *Holiday,* to write a play for her. He concocted *The Philadelphia Story*, and she had herself an unqualified Broadway hit. Hepburn had waived part of her fee for partial ownership in the play. Consequently, when MGM made the movie version, they had to cast her as the lead. Thus, Hepburn learned to take control of her career in ways that were unique for her time.

Following the phenomenal success of *The Philadelphia Story*, Hepburn was riding high in Hollywood. She used the leverage to make several demands on MGM. First, she wanted to make *Woman of the Year* (she'd commissioned the Oscar-winning script from Ring

Grand Old Man of the movies." A Broadway actor when he was signed by Fox in 1930, he wasn't really established in films until 1933, when he appeared in *20,000 Years in Sing Sing*. He was signed by MGM in 1935, and in the following few years won two Oscars for *Captains Courageous* and *Boys Town*. (He holds the

In *Woman of the Year* Hepburn matches Tracy drink for drink, bragging that she's never wound up under the table—except in this case, where she ducks down to retrieve the contents of her purse. "You're wonderful," Tracy tells Hepburn. "Of course," replies the ever-confident Hepburn, "didn't you know?" She was one lady who knew how to take a compliment.

record for the most Best Actor nominations—nine.) By 1940, he was more popular at the box office than Clark Gable. He was adored by the public and critics alike for his sincerity, his forthright manliness, and his totally natural and seemingly effortless performances. Hepburn expressed the general consensus among actors in describing Tracy's acting genius: "He never gussied it up. He just did it, he let it ride along on its enormous simplicity. That's what was absolutely thrilling about Spencer's acting." Among his peers, he was known as the "Prince of Underplayers."

James Cagney once observed that nightclub entertainers were always doing impressions of "Eddie Robinson, me, Bogie, Jimmy Stewart, John Wayne. Have you ever noticed they never imitate Spence? Never try? You know why that is? It's because there's nothing to imitate except his genius and that can't be mimicked. He doesn't have any mannerisms of his own. Well, maybe that jaw clench but that's nerves, I think, more than anything. You know, *squeezing* the part out. With him every character he plays develops his own mannerisms and idiosyncrasies."

When once asked about the secret to his talent, Tracy replied that "the art of acting is—learn your lines."

Tracy was well known in Hollywood to be a big drinker. "He was afraid of going on a bender," wrote Myrna Loy, who costarred with him in such films as *Libeled Lady* and *Test Pilot*. "He'd had a drinking problem for some years; one drink could set him off. It was a real problem and he knew it, but he had the discipline to abstain during shooting. Between pictures, sometimes, he would just disappear for a spell, but not while he worked."

He also had a reputation as a womanizer and, over the years, repeatedly made passes at Loy, which she never returned. One day, he arrived at her hotel room after he'd been on a bender. She recalled: "He made the usual play for me . . . then he turned defensive. 'You don't have to worry about me anymore,' Tracy said like a sulky child. 'I've found the woman I want.' As he outlined the virtues of Katharine Hepburn, I was relieved, but a little disappointed. As selfish as it sounds, I liked having a man like Spence in the background waiting for me."

An open secret in Hollywood, the alliance between Tracy and Hepburn was to last for the next twenty-six years. Tracy was married to the former stage actress Louise Treadwell, and, though they never divorced, they lived apart for many years. He made his home in hotel suites. "I've always liked to live in small places," he once told Garson Kanin, "because I live a small life." Tracy and Hepburn were seldom seen without each other, except when they were working on location in different parts of the world. Everyone knew about their relationship, but in deference to the respected couple even Hollywood gossip columnists didn't write about them.

From Tracy and Hepburn's very first screen appearance together, it was clear they were meant for each other. In *Woman of the Year,* they play dueling reporters who fall in love. But she's an independent woman not looking for marriage. When he proposes she hesitates, saying: "Always swore I wouldn't. The frightening idea of getting tied down. Guess there's one thing I didn't figure on—you." Unlike most women of her day, Hepburn didn't need to be married, but she needed Tracy.

The movie was a resounding success. In *Time* James Agee wrote: "Actors Hepburn and Tracy have a fine old time in *Woman of the Year*. They take turns playing straight for each other. . . . As a lady columnist, she's just right. As a working reporter, he's practically perfect. For once strident Katharine Hepburn is properly subdued." Tracy would perform this same deed in many of their films: he would subdue her without squelching her spirit.

The *Baltimore Sun* emphasized that Tracy's "quiet masculine stubbornness and prosaic outlook on life is in striking contrast with her sparkle and brilliance. They make a fine team, and each complements the other." And the *New York Herald-Tribune* declared: "Hepburn and Tracy play the leading roles with such skill and gusto that it becomes irresistibly entertaining."

The pair's second picture together, *Keeper of the Flame,* served to solidify them as a team. Ironically, it's the only movie in which they're not a couple and they don't wind up together. In it, Hepburn has to die to

Opposite:
Once she accepts his proposal, Hepburn wants to run off to get married in *Woman of the Year*, but Tracy prefers a more traditional wedding. Though dressed in the right clothes, their ceremony lasts only a few moments, after which she rushes off to take an important call. Such a reversal of traditional male/female sentiments was a hallmark of many Tracy/Hepburn collaborations.

In *Keeper of the Flame*, an obscure political drama, war journalist Tracy wants to write a book about widow Hepburn's late husband, an American hero. At first, she refuses to help Tracy but then changes her mind and, ultimately, tells him that her husband fronted for a Fascist organization that wanted to take over the world by stirring up hatred and racism. Though she's killed for her efforts to expose the organization, her death is not in vain. Tracy writes his book and denounces the bad guys.

make the country safe for democracy. The switch from comedy to drama didn't serve them well, but the fault rested more with the weak script and the convoluted plot. At one point Tracy says: "I'm a little lost," and Hepburn replies: "I'm lost, too." So was the audience. Years later, director George Cukor confessed, "I don't think I really believed in the story, it was pure hokey-

pokey. . . . Everyone looked like a waxwork in Madame Tussaud's." Yet, in spite of its weaknesses, this film remains interesting for the quality of the acting. Neither Tracy nor Hepburn ever shows a false emotion, even given the unworkable material.

They were on surer ground in their next film, *Without Love*, which had been adapted from a Philip

Barry play in which Hepburn had starred on Broadway. In this film Hepburn is a woman "who's kept a lot of things locked up for a lot of years." She's shy and scared of people. She says: "I pray for guidance and blush when I get it." He's a "high-brow scientist" who "hasn't cracked a smile in years." He prefers books to people because "a book doesn't double-cross you." He needs a place to conduct his wartime experiments and takes over the basement of her house in Washington, D.C. She offers to assist him, and their working arrangement is so successful they agree to marry, strictly for the sake of companionship. No sex. No love. No muss, no fuss. By the last reel, of course, they renege on their deal.

Without Love set the formula for a number of their subsequent films, containing several ingredients essential to a successful Tracy-Hepburn vehicle. Older people, each settled in their own ways, they are resigned to their generally lonely lot in life. They meet through some kind of working arrangement, and slowly come to realize they have similar tastes and interests. They fall in love, without knowing or acknowledging it. He draws her out, she helps him work, and, in the process, they make each other more vulnerable, more human.

In 1948 Tracy was signed to star in *State of the Union* with Claudette Colbert, but at the last minute she fought with the studio about her working hours. Hepburn happily replaced Colbert as the estranged

In *Without Love*, Hepburn doesn't know that Tracy sleepwalks when she allows him to move into her Washington home to conduct wartime experiments. The premise allowed for some pajama-clad scenes, which was about as risqué as Tracy and Hepburn ever got in their work together.

Soon, she's assisting him with his experiments, and they agree to marry, strictly for convenience and companionship. As always, their relationship is based on mutual admiration: she's awed by his brilliance; he's taken by her grasp of his scientific mumbo-jumbo. Of course, they eventually fall in love.

Opposite:
When Hepburn proposes marriage in *Without Love,* Tracy replies: "You're nuts." Undaunted, Hepburn counters: "So are you." Of course, they were perfectly suited to each other, and their movies extolled the virtues of marriage based on mutual respect, similar interests, and companionship.

Above:
Adapted from a story by Conrad Richter, *The Sea of Grass* was the only Old West movie Tracy and Hepburn made, and it remains one of their lesser-known features. Tracy plays a ruthless cattle baron and Hepburn is his sensitive wife. The movie received good reviews, but was a box-office failure.

wife of businessman Tracy. Drafted to run for president, he needs Hepburn at his side. She agrees to help him, hoping their relationship will improve. (He's having an affair with Angela Lansbury.)

In one speech, Hepburn acknowledges both her admiration for and frustration with Tracy: "I know he's a big man. You know he's a big man. My bad days are when he knows he's a big man. Isn't there any way of Grant's being elected president and keeping it a secret from him?"

She also defines the differences between them: "Grant needs a lot of room to stretch in. He likes to get up on those mountaintops and slap the hurricanes down. He can do it, too. He began to feel I was sort of small potatoes and holding him back. I was, I guess. I'm a cozy corner person. . . . I like those quiet valleys."

The differences between Tracy and Hepburn on screen were similar to those off. "The surprising aspect of their joint success was that they were so different," writes Garson Kanin. "Kate's working method and approach was opposite Spencer's. She is a careful, thorough, methodical, analytical, concentrated artist. She reads and studies and thinks. By the time she was ready to begin shooting *The Lion in Winter,* for example, she knew enough about Eleanor of Aquitaine to write a master's thesis on the subject. She loves to rehearse and practice and try things and make just one more take.

"Spencer, conversely, was an instinctive player, who trusted the moment of creation, believed it was possible to go stale by overrehearsing, and usually did his best work on the first take. He was a firmly rooted subjective artist."

Though they were different, they succeeded as a couple because they were both dedicated and devoted to honesty. In *State of the Union* Hepburn lays the foundation of their relationship by telling Tracy: "One way or another, things should be clean and honest between us."

Opposite:
"If I throw my hat in the ring, does my head go with it?"
asks businessman Tracy before deciding
to make a bid for the presidency in *State of the Union*.
To win, he needs help from his estranged wife, Hepburn.
Though she resents being used, Hepburn agrees to
masquerade as his dutiful wife. Naturally, she's totally
believable in the role.

Hepburn and Tracy play strong-headed lawyers in *Adam's Rib* who wind up on opposite sides of a major case. "You're aging fast," she tells him. "You're helping," he counters.

Honesty, by way of equality, was fundamental to Tracy and Hepburn, and none of their movies is more devoted to this idea than *Adam's Rib*. The movie addresses the theme of equality in both its plot and in the relationship between its leads. Both are lawyers on opposing sides of a case involving a wife who shoots her husband after catching him with a woman.

Hepburn asks a prospective juror: "Do you believe in equal rights for women?" "I should say not," he indignantly scoffs. Hepburn makes a plea for equality. "For years women have been ridiculed, pampered, and chucked under the chin," she tells the jury. "I ask you, be fair to the fair sex."

Then, she carries her crusade home. She demands that Tracy treat her with respect and equality, redefining their relationship in remarkably contemporary terms: "Marriage, what it's supposed to be . . . what makes it work or perfect . . . balance, equality, mutual every-

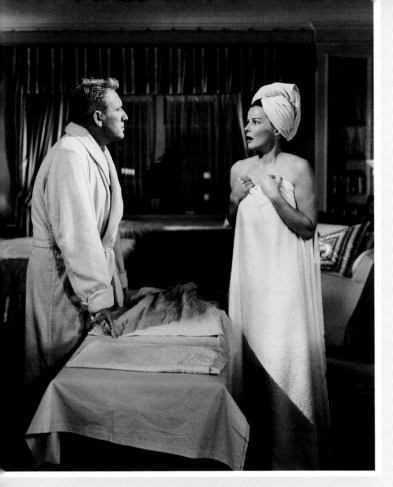

Opposite and above:
In *Adam's Rib* Tracy and Hepburn argue with the judge while playing footsie underneath the desk in court. Unable to leave their differing legal opinions in the courtroom, they are soon battling it out with each other at home.

thing. There's no room in marriage for what used to be known as the little woman. She's got to be as big as the man is . . . sharing . . . that's what it takes to make a marriage, keep a marriage from getting sick of all the duties and responsibilities and troubles. . . . Listen, no part of marriage is the exclusive province of any one sex. . . ."

The theme of equality of the sexes is repeated in their next two films. In *Pat and Mike,* she's a star athlete and he's a sports promoter. "What's good for you, is good for me and you for me, see?" Tracy tells Hepburn. "We're the same, we're equal, we're partners. See? Five–oh, five–oh." In the final scene, they agree to marry or, more aptly, to merge:

TRACY:	I don't know if I can lick you or you can lick me, but I tell you one thing I do know, together we can lick them all.
HEPBURN:	You bet.
TRACY:	I can't handle this in my head. It rocks me.
HEPBURN:	Why?
TRACY:	It don't figure. . . . I mean, there's one thing about us hooking together that's what I call a plenty long shot.
HEPBURN:	Nothing wrong with a long shot.
TRACY:	If you come out on top, that's a fact.
HEPBURN:	We will Mike.
TRACY:	You don't seem to . . . an upper cruster like you and a . . . my kind of type that can't even speak left-handed English . . .the whole gizmo it's hard for me to believe.
HEPBURN:	Not hard for me to believe.
TRACY:	I think so.
HEPBURN:	I know so.
TRACY:	Okay, kid, you got yourself a deal. (*They shake hands.*)

In *Desk Set*, he's a computer genius, and she runs the research department of a media corporation. The premise allows for their trademark no-nonsense courting; it's all vital statistics, at least on the surface:

HEPBURN:	I've read every New York newspaper backward and forward for the past fifteen years. I don't smoke, I only drink champagne when I'm lucky enough to get it. My hair is naturally natural. I live alone and so do you.
TRACY:	How do you know that?
HEPBURN:	Because you're wearing one brown sock and one black one. . . . If you lived with anyone, they would've told you.
TRACY:	That's one of the advantages of living alone, no one tells you anything.

He proceeds to give her a test, challenging her with brain twisters and advising her to "never assume." She doesn't, matching him twister for twister, until he concludes she's "a very rare tropical fish." He proposes to her by computer.

In the early '60s, Tracy became gravely ill, and Hepburn retired from films for several years to nurse him. In 1966 they began working on their last collaboration,

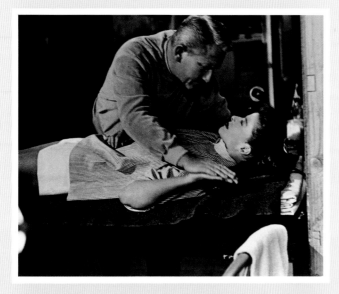

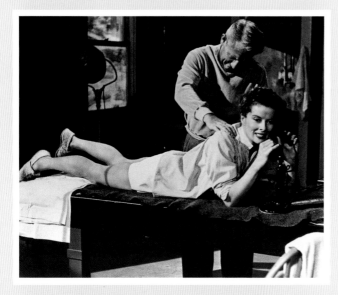

In *Pat and Mike* Tracy is a sports promoter with a heavy Brooklyn accent and Hepburn's a high-class socialite with natural athletic abilities. "Not much meat on her," he says, "but what's there is choice." Here, in a typical, no-nonsense love scene, physical therapy takes on a whole new aura when Tracy gives Hepburn a massage after a strenuous workout.

Guess Who's Coming to Dinner. Though they were noticeably older and Tracy looked frail and ill, the power of their personal and professional connection was obvious. A long-married couple, their only daughter (played by Hepburn's niece Katharine Houghton) falls in love with a black man (Sidney Poitier). If Tracy and Hepburn don't give their approval to the match within one day's time, Poitier will leave for Switzerland without Houghton.

In one scene, Hepburn talks about her screen marriage to Tracy: "For us it's all been great, but you know what was the best time of all? Was in the beginning, when everything was a struggle, and you were working too hard and worried and sometimes frightened, and there were times when I felt, when I really knew, that I was a help to you. That was the very best time of all for me."

Three weeks after they finished filming *Guess Who's Coming to Dinner* Tracy died at the age of sixty-seven.

Both actors were nominated for Oscars for the film, but only Hepburn won. "I always felt they gave it (the Oscar) to both of us," she later said. She didn't attend the ceremonies, but the next day sent the following telegram to Gregory Peck, then president of the academy:

"IT WAS DELIGHTFUL A TOTAL SURPRISE. I AM ENORMOUSLY TOUCHED BECAUSE I FEEL I HAVE RECEIVED A GREAT AFFECTIONATE HUG FROM MY FELLOW WORKERS AND FOR A VARIETY OF REASONS NOT THE LEAST OF WHICH BEING SPENCER STANLEY SIDNEY KATHY AND BILL ROSE. ROSE WROTE ABOUT A NORMAL MIDDLE AGED UNSPECTACULAR UNGLAMOROUS CREATURE WITH A GOOD BRAIN AND A WARM HEART WHO'S DOING THE BEST SHE CAN TO DO THE DECENT THING IN A DIFFICULT SITUATION. IN OTHER WORDS SHE WAS A GOOD WIFE. OUR MOST UNSUNG AND IMPORTANT HEROINE. I'M GLAD SHE'S COMING BACK IN STYLE. I MODELED HER AFTER MY MOTHER. THANKS AGAIN. THEY DON'T USUALLY GIVE THESE THINGS TO THE OLD GIRLS YOU KNOW."

Perhaps not, although during the course of her long career, Hepburn has won an unprecedented four Oscars for Best Actress. Despite such achievements she once remarked: "I would've loved to (have been) a writer or a painter . . . anything I could've done alone. I would've liked to have had a more private life."

She's worked hard to retain her privacy, always refusing to discuss her personal relationship with Tracy.

The research library was the perfect setting for a Tracy/Hepburn love scene in *Desk Set*, where he compares Hepburn to his beloved computer: "You're both singleminded, you go on relentlessly trying to get the answer." Hepburn wants to know what happens if the computer can't find the answer, and Tracy replies: "If she becomes frustrated, her magnetic circuit is liable to go off." Hepburn understands. "Something like that is happening to me," she observes.

She made perhaps her most revealing comment about him in a television interview: "He found life difficult. He found living difficult and being fair difficult. He found acting easy. He could just do it. He was the most entertaining creature. Wonderful storyteller."

At the conclusion of *Guess Who's Coming to Dinner*, Tracy delivers a long speech, summing up the film's story line and, perhaps, his offscreen relationship with Hepburn as well: "Mrs. Prentice (Poitier's mother) says that like her husband, I'm a burnt-out old shell of a man who cannot even remember what it's like to love a woman. . . . You're wrong as you can be. . . . I know exactly how he feels about her, and there's nothing, absolutely nothing, that your son feels for my daughter

that I didn't feel for Christina (Hepburn). Old? Yes. Burnt-out? Certainly. But I can tell you the memories are still there. Clear. Intact. Indestructible. And they'll be there if I live to be 110. Where John (Poitier) made his mistake, I think, was in attaching so much importance to what her mother and I might think. . . . The only thing that matters is what they feel and how much they feel for each other. And if it's half of what we felt, that's everything. . . ."

His voice cracks. Tears well up in her eyes. The camera catches him staring at her. It's one of the most immediate and poignant moments ever captured on film. Everyone in the audience knows Tracy is talking about his years with Hepburn.

When he finishes his speech, she strides over to him and shakes his hand. Totally consistent with their relationship on screen and off, it's a vintage Tracy-Hepburn gesture.

Opposite and above:
Tracy and Hepburn in *Guess Who's Coming to Dinner,* their final film together. Both actors had aged considerably in the twenty-five years since they first costarred, but neither age nor ill health detracted from their magnetism on screen.
If anything, Tracy seems even more accessible and powerful as an actor, and Hepburn's far-from-faded beauty gives credence to the adage that after forty years of age, a woman gets the face she deserves.

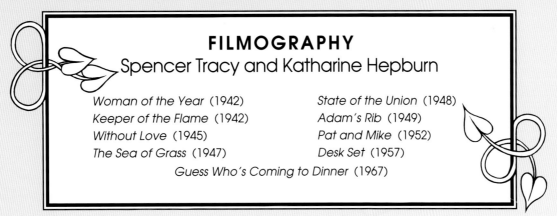

FILMOGRAPHY
Spencer Tracy and Katharine Hepburn

Woman of the Year (1942)

Keeper of the Flame (1942)

Without Love (1945)

The Sea of Grass (1947)

State of the Union (1948)

Adam's Rib (1949)

Pat and Mike (1952)

Desk Set (1957)

Guess Who's Coming to Dinner (1967)

ALLEN & KEATON

"A certain type of woman likes me.
The type that has cut her wrists at least once.
I appeal to women in proportion to the times they have attempted suicide."

WOODY ALLEN, interview in the *Los Angeles Times*

In countless ways, Woody Allen is the most extraordinary filmmaker in America. Certainly, he is unique. Over the past two decades, no one else has produced a more diversified and original body of work. And Allen is the only actor who has made his best films with his real-life partners. His second wife, Louise Lasser, starred in two early movies and, with the exception of *Everything You Always Wanted to Know About Sex* and *Stardust Memories,* all his own films since *Play It Again, Sam* have starred either Diane Keaton or Mia Farrow.

Though not married to either woman, he has had long-term relationships with both: with Keaton from 1972 to 1979, and with Farrow since 1982. He has generously praised them in terms of how they have enriched his work: "I feel like I've lucked out working with Diane Keaton and Mia. . . . They've made this contribution to me. My contribution is relatively minimal. I can only provide the script and then they bail me out, they make me look good."

But certainly they've had good material to work with. As a writer and director with autonomous control over his work, Woody Allen can create personalized vehicles for his leading women. "When I know a person intimately, I can write nuances and subtleties into a character that I want her to play," he has said.

Opposite and right:
In *Annie Hall,* Diane Keaton and Woody Allen are a perfectly mismatched couple. She eats pastrami on white bread with tomatoes and mayo, and he claims to be among the few males suffering from penis envy. Despite their differences, or maybe because of them, they are wildly attracted to each other when they first get together. "Love is too weak a word for what I feel," he tells her. "I *lurve* you. I *luff* you."

Though a few married couples work together in somewhat similar ways—Blake Edwards writes for and directs his wife, Julie Andrews; Neil Simon wrote several movies for his former wife Marsha Mason; and the late

John Cassavetes wrote for, directed, and sometimes starred with his wife, Gena Rowlands—none of these filmmakers has made as many movies with a single partner as has Allen.

The story ideas and plot lines for Allen's films are kept in the strictest confidence by everyone on his set. Few people know anything about his films until they are released to the public. Allen demands privacy in his personal life as well. He rarely grants interviews and does not appear on talk shows. He is rarely photographed.

Allen has argued that his screen characters are not autobiographical, but no one accepts this. In a review of *Annie Hall* in the *New Yorker*, Penelope Gilliatt wrote: "The hero is called Alvy Singer but biographically and neurotically he could pass for Woody Allen any day." Ironically, his portrayal of relationships and the conflicts between what we need and what we get from love and sex touches such profound chords in his audience that most people assume his films are simply reenactments of his life. This is why, for example, so much press was given to the fact that many scenes from *Hannah and Her Sisters* were shot in Farrow's apartment on Central Park. How intimate it felt to see the place where Allen spends time with Farrow—almost like an invitation to dinner with the couple. Of course, this is an illusion. We may think we know him, but we do not. And, truthfully, we don't need to. Allen's films stand on their own, no matter how much Annie Hall is really Diane Keaton or Hannah is really, as Allen once said, "a romanticized version of Mia Farrow."

No filmmaker better understands how much we are influenced by movies than Woody Allen. All his work is filled with references to other films. In *Play It Again, Sam* Allen's wife tells him: "You like movies because you're one of life's watchers." Indeed, in many of his films, Allen plays a character who constantly goes to the movies. In *Annie Hall* he is obsessed with seeing *The Sorrow and the Pity*, a 4 1/2-hour documentary about the French resistance to the Nazis, over and over. He can't bear to miss one second, not even the opening credits. "But they're in Swedish," wails Keaton. It doesn't matter. "I have to see a movie from start to finish 'cause I'm anal," he tells her.

In *Manhattan* Allen watches *Grand Illusion* and W. C. Fields movies while in bed with Mariel Hemingway. In *Crimes and Misdemeanors* he tells his niece: "I promised your father on his death bed that I would give you a rounded education, so we probably shouldn't go to the movies every day."

In Allen's world, filled as it is with angst and uncertainty, movies are an anchor. Thus, in *The Purple Rose of Cairo*, when the movie-within-the-movie is altered because Jeff Daniels steps off the screen and into the arms of Mia Farrow, a woman in the audience cries: "I just saw this movie last week; this is not what happens. I want what happened last week to happen—otherwise what's life about anyway?" Indeed, movies don't just imitate life for Woody Allen; movies are life—and a kind of religion. In *Radio Days* he recalls "the first time I ever saw Radio City Music Hall. . . . It was like entering heaven."

In *Hannah and Her Sisters*, Allen pulls himself out of a suicidal depression by watching a Marx Brothers movie: "I'm watching these people on the screen and I started getting hooked on the film, you know, and I started to feel: how could you even think of killing yourself? I mean . . . look at all the people up there on the screen. They're real funny, and what if the worst is true? What if there is no God, and you only go around once, and that's it? Well, don't you want to be part of the experience?" Ultimately, Allen endows movies with a lifesaving grace, finding in film the mystical experience he doesn't find elsewhere: movies provide the impetus for him to go on living. It's no coincidence then that this multitalented writer, who could have worked in almost any media (and has, in fact, written several Broadway plays and collections of short stories), has dedicated himself to making films.

Allen was born in Brooklyn in 1935. "I'm relatively normal for a guy raised in Brooklyn," says Alvy Singer in *Annie Hall*. Never much of a student, Allen once told *Rolling Stone:* "I loathe and regret every day I spent in school. I like to be taught to read and write and then be left alone." At the age of fifteen he sold jokes to syndicated newspapers and, flunking out of New York University, began writing for television at the age of eighteen.

At the age of twenty-two, Allen was earning $1,500 a week writing gags for Garry Moore. ("If only I had the nerve to do my own jokes," muses Alvy, a comedy writer.) Ultimately, Allen left his job in TV to work as a stand-up comedian, taking home perhaps $150 a week. But not for long. Within two years, he commanded $10,000 a night as one of the hottest comics in the country.

His comedy was something new; he was the ill-at-ease urban everyman who openly shared his neuroses. As Paul D. Zimmerman wrote in *Time:* "Allen's great comic strength lies in his willingness to dramatize his most intimate psychological tensions, to exaggerate them for comic effect, of course, but . . . (also to) summon the laughter of recognition in each of us."

His first venture into movies was his rewrite of the screenplay for *What's New, Pussycat?,* which broke box-office records for a comedy. (He was, however, devastated by the final film. "They butchered my script," he told *Boston After Dark*.) His next film, *What's Up, Tiger Lily?,* a James Bond spoof that dubbed English dialogue over a cheap Japanese thriller, became a cult classic. In 1969 Allen directed and starred in *Take the Money and Run,* a movie he cowrote with Mickey Rose. Two years later, he did the same thing for *Bananas* (a favorite among his fans). After both these films proved to be box-office hits, Allen was able to make movies with more freedom from studio interference.

At best, he was an unlikely movie star. Short and gawky, he was klutzy and tongue-tied around women. He dressed in crumpled army fatigues, wore his trademark nerdy glasses, and refused to disguise his thinning red hair. He was as far away from the leading men of the late sixties—Warren Beatty, Sean Connery, Ryan O'Neal, and Robert Redford—as any man could be. But instead of trying to improve or glamorize his physical traits, Allen used them for comic effect. In fact, he played them to the hilt in his first film with Diane Keaton, *Play It Again, Sam.*

Left, top and bottom:
In *Manhattan* Woody Allen plays a successful but neurotic television writer who falls for Diane Keaton, his best friend's mistress. She's intensely insecure. "Your self-esteem is a notch above Kafka," Allen tells her. But they relate to each other because he, too, has problems with love.
"There must be something wrong with me because I've never had a relationship that's lasted longer than the one between Hitler and Eva Braun," claims Allen. Still, Keaton and Allen attempt a relationship, making the traditional New York dating scene: visiting an art museum and running through Central Park in the rain.
Overleaf:
Yet, perhaps *Manhattan* is more about Woody Allen's love affair with the city than with any woman, as these beautifully photographed cityscapes suggest.

183

In *Sleeper* Woody Allen is shocked to discover that everyone he knows has been dead for 200 years. "But they all ate brown rice," he wails, confused and bewildered. "I don't know what I'm doing here. I'm 237 years old, I should be collecting social security." *Sleeper* deftly mixed rapid one-liners with stylish slapstick. "I'm always joking, you know that. It's a defense mechanism," explains Allen to Keaton, as if he needed an excuse for his brilliant wit.

Here, he's the ultimate loser with women. When his wife (Susan Anspach) leaves him, he despairs of ever finding another woman. "I managed to fool one woman into loving me, and now she's gone," he tells Keaton, the wife of his best friend (Tony Roberts).

Though Keaton is sympathetic, she does have to wonder: "Don't you think it was a little strange, he was married and he still couldn't get a date on New Year's Eve?"

As in most of their early films, Allen is the ultimate nebbish, and Keaton the unattainable goddess of his dreams. Yet she falls for him, learning to appreciate the qualities he doesn't show other women. They go to bed together, and afterward have what was to become a typical Allen–Keaton postcoital exchange. "You were wonderful last night. . . . How do you feel now?" he asks. "I think the Pepto-Bismol really helped," she replies. (When they kiss at the end of *Sleeper*, he says: "Sex and death. Two things that come once in a lifetime, but at least after death, you're not nauseous.")

Keaton was Allen's perfect costar in the '70s. They met when she auditioned for the Broadway production of *Play It Again, Sam*. Born Diane Hall in Los Angeles in 1946, she came to New York at the age of nineteen to study acting. On Broadway, she appeared in the original production of *Hair* (1968) before landing the lead in *Play It Again, Sam*. She made two movies in the early 1970s—*Lovers and Other Strangers* and *The Godfather*—but made her mark as Allen's offbeat leading woman.

In Allen's futuristic spoof *Sleeper* she plays the empty-headed Luna to Allen's milquetoast Myles Monroe. Wrapped in aluminum foil and frozen in a capsule in 1973, Allen is defrosted two centuries later. "It's hard to believe you haven't had sex in 200 years," Keaton remarks. He concurs but corrects her: "204, if you count my marriage."

Their next film, *Love and Death*, parodies *War and Peace* by way of Fellini, and Keaton plays an airhead who is half saint, half whore. Again, her main function is to feed him the straight lines. "Sex without love is an empty experience," she tells him. "Yes," he agrees, "but as empty experiences go, it's one of the best."

Though the settings for Allen's movies with Keaton vary widely, they always play essentially the same characters. Keaton is the quintessential WASP beauty to Allen's urban Jewish neurotic, although Allen protests this description. "I don't have that Jewish obsession," Allen commented in 1976. "I use my background when it's expedient for me in my work. But it's not really an obsession of mine, and I never had that obsession with Gentile women."

Whatever his type or his preference, certainly Allen utilized Keaton's WASP qualities in their most famous collaboration, *Annie Hall*. Beautiful but uneducated, she's the opposite of Allen's Alvy Singer. The intellectual Allen coaxes her to read books with the word *death* in the title. Her well-bred family discusses swap meets and boating over Easter dinner. "Where did you grow up, in a Norman Rockwell painting?" Allen asks her. In contrast, Alvy Singer grew up under the roller coaster in Coney Island, where dinner conversations revolved around such topics as diabetes and coronaries.

Critics have, of course, noted that Allen used Keaton's real last name in the title of the movie, claiming this proved the movie was autobiographical.

Jack Hall, Diane Keaton's father, said about the film: "It's 85 percent true—even to (my wife) Dorothy and my mother." But Allen told Garson Kanin that "eighty percent of the film is fabricated."

The controversy misses the point. *Annie Hall* became a classic, sweeping the Oscars for Best Actress, Best Original Screenplay, Best Direction, and Best Picture not because of Allen and Keaton's real lives but because of their relationship on screen. They are the archetypal, enigmatic couple of the '70s—madly in love and seriously in trouble, doubtful yet hopeful, wanting love to last forever but knowing it can't, trying desperately to establish a sense of permanence but constantly changing. They discuss highbrow topics such as art and photography while, in subtitles, he wonders what she looks like naked and she worries that "he probably thinks I'm a yo-yo."

Until just weeks before its release, *Annie Hall* was titled *Anhedonia* (a psychological term for the lack of pleasure or of the capacity to seek it). Allen has, on occasion, described himself as anhedonic. Many of the conflicts between Annie and Alvy revolve around this failure to enjoy life's bounties, to take joy from love. "You are incapable of enjoying life," Annie tells Alvy during an argument.

Every aspect of their relationship represents some kind of conflict—and how familiar they are to us! He wants her to be better educated, but doesn't want her to change. He wants her to live with him, but doesn't want her to give up her own apartment. She wants to be loving, but can't make love to him. She wants to be independent, but allows him to pay for her therapy. She wants to be with him, but wants to meet other people. Perfectly mismatched, they must work at every aspect of their relationship; in order to solve a problem, they must turn to their respective shrinks.

At the first sign of crisis, both threaten to jump ship. She breaks up with him after he becomes jealous of her college professor. Then, she calls in the middle of the night and they resume their affair, without much success. "A relationship is like a shark," he tells her. "It has to constantly move forward or it dies. What we have here is a dead shark." He breaks up with her and then, only a few months later, begs her to return.

There are few happy endings in Allen's movies. Except for *Sleeper*, he and Keaton never wind up together at the end of the film. "It's never something you did,

Allen wrote the script for, directed, but did not appear in *Interiors,* his first attempt at a serious film. Diane Keaton (above, with Allen) plays a poet in analysis who, along with her sisters (Marybeth Hurt and Kristin Griffith), must deal with the traumatic divorce of their parents (E. G. Marshall and Geraldine Page) and the repercussions of Marshall's remarriage to Maureen Stapleton. The story of this desperately unhappy family reminded many critics of Ingmar Bergman, and many of Allen's fans were upset when Allen abandoned comedy for such intense drama. Still, *Interiors* is a deeply compelling and heartfelt film, certainly a major triumph in its own right.

people change. Love fades," a lady on the street reminds Alvy. And perhaps this was the key to the success of the film, as Allen himself said in an interview: "I guess what everybody understood (about the film) was the impossibility of sustaining relationships, because of entirely irrational elements. . . . Later in life, you really don't know what went wrong." In *Sleeper* Keaton explains why meaningful relationships between men and women don't last: "There's a chemical in our bodies that makes it so we get on each other's nerves sooner or later."

But Annie and Alvy remain friends. At the end of the film, they meet for lunch to discuss old times, and, as she walks away from him, he is reminded of that old joke about the guy who goes to a psychotherapist because his brother thinks he's a chicken. When the shrink asks why he doesn't commit the brother, the guy replies: "I would, but I need the eggs." And that's how Allen feels about relationships: "You know, they're totally irrational and crazy and absurd, but I guess we keep going through it because most of us need the eggs."

Allen made *Manhattan*, his last film with Keaton, in 1979. Still needing the eggs, Allen's character says: "People should mate for life, like penguins or Catholics." (This same joke pops up eleven years later in *Alice*, when Farrow tells her Chinese doctor she's been fantasizing about penguins "because they mate for life." Annoyed, the doctor says: "You think penguins are Catholics.")

But in *Manhattan*, again, lifetime mating is not possible for Allen. "I'm dating a girl who does homework," he tells his friend about seventeen-year-old Mariel Hemingway. Though she's too young for him, she loves him with a maturity far beyond her years: "We have laughs together. I care about you. Your concerns are my concerns. We have great sex." Who could ask for more? Anhedonic Allen, of course.

He dumps Hemingway for Keaton, the "winner of the Zelda Fitzgerald Emotional Maturity Award." Keaton has been dating married Michael Murphy, Allen's best friend. Yet Allen is drawn to her; they are inevitable—until they live together and discover, just as in *Annie Hall*, that they are completely incompatible. She leaves him to return to Murphy.

Allen is despondent, yet the movie ends on a note of optimism. He rediscovers his love for Hemingway and rushes to her. We don't know if they wind up together, but that's not the point. "You've got to have a little faith in people," Hemingway tells Allen. Even though a relationship between Keaton and Allen seems nearly impossible, things may work out between him and another woman. Just admitting that, with a little faith, love is possible seemed a major new direction for Allen, and was consistent with the transformation of his screen character since *Play It Again, Sam*. He had gone from the nebbish who fools women into loving him to the man who, though still neurotic, has a choice of women but instinctively gravitates toward the wrong one. He had changed a lot more than Keaton, who essentially played the same woman in all of Allen's films. In *Manhattan* she was still the anxiety-ridden, unattainable, anhedonic beauty, constantly tripping over her own feet, unable to make a commitment or sustain a relationship. Perhaps Keaton was playing herself, or perhaps Allen could only see her in this one role. Certainly, in the films she made following her breakup with Allen—*Reds*, *Shoot the Moon*, and *Crimes of the Heart*, for example—she expanded her palette as an actress. As for Allen, he needed a costar who had a wider range within the framework of his vision, and he found her in Mia Farrow.

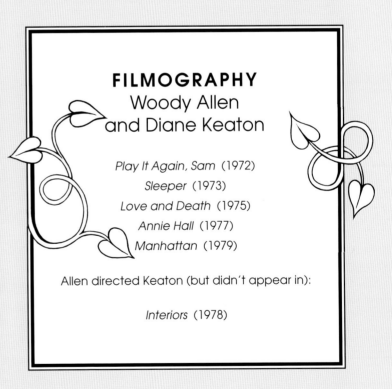

FILMOGRAPHY
Woody Allen
and Diane Keaton

Play It Again, Sam (1972)
Sleeper (1973)
Love and Death (1975)
Annie Hall (1977)
Manhattan (1979)

Allen directed Keaton (but didn't appear in):

Interiors (1978)

ALLEN & FARROW

"I could go on about our differences forever. . . .
(Mia) has raised nine children with no trauma and has never owned a thermometer.
I take my temperature every two hours in the course of the day."

WOODY ALLEN, interview in the *New York Times* (February 24, 1991)

Woody Allen and Mia Farrow first met at a party in California, when he was with Diane Keaton and Farrow was married to André Previn. In 1980 he saw her again, and they started dating. A few months later they were working together.

Farrow had lived an extraordinary life before she met Allen. The daughter of film director John Farrow and actress Maureen O'Sullivan, she grew up among Hollywood royalty. But Farrow won her first acting job in an open casting call, having been picked out of a line of fifty girls before the producers even knew her name. The part she won in *The Importance of Being Earnest* led to a contract with 20th Century-Fox and a starring role in the new TV series, "Peyton Place." At the age of nineteen, she achieved superstardom.

A year later, in 1966, she married fifty-year-old Frank Sinatra. Radio and TV stations interrupted regular programming for special bulletins on their elopement to Las Vegas. She became a gossip columnist's dream; her every action was publicized. She made headlines across the country when she had her long hair cropped short. Then, she starred in *Rosemary's Baby,* a worldwide hit that enhanced her reputation as a serious actress. She was only twenty-two years old.

She divorced Sinatra, went to India with the Beatles, studied with a guru, and returned to London in order to resume her career. She had twin boys with

Opposite:
Woody Allen is madly in love with Mia Farrow in *Crimes and Misdemeanors.* Though they are perfectly suited to each other, he loses her to Alan Alda, which serves to confirm the semi-serious advice that Allen gives to his niece in this film: "You'll find as you go through life that great depth and smoldering sensuality doesn't always win, I'm sorry to say."

conductor André Previn before he divorced his wife to marry her. Then the couple adopted four more children. She worked on stage and played opposite Robert Redford in *The Great Gatsby* (1974). After divorcing Previn, Farrow adopted another child on her own.

Her first movie with Allen was *A Midsummer Night's Sex Comedy* (1982); he cast her as Ariel Weymouth, a beautiful, innocent-looking, Victorian nymphomaniac. "Originally, I asked Mia to work with me because we were going out and I thought it would be fun," Allen has said. "I've discovered through our working together that she's easy to work with. . . . And she has a great sense of believability. You can give her anything to do and she will make it real."

She was nervous about working with him, saying: "I was afraid that I would disappoint someone who was a friend and whom I cared about. . . . I was afraid I wouldn't be good enough and inevitably would disappoint."

Far from it. Allen has found amazingly varied ways to utilize her talents. In essence, Farrow seems to represent a female version of Allen's own screen persona, especially as he appeared in his early films. She has nontraditional looks and deportment. Though she can be astonishingly beautiful, she can also look frumpy and ill at ease in her own skin. Her screen characters are, much like Allen's, often shy and awkward. On screen, Farrow speaks with Allenesque intonations and stutterings. She often stumbles over her sentences, giving the impression she's not quite sure what she's going to say next. She's plagued by insecurity, both on screen and off. She told film critic Roger Ebert: "I always worry I won't be any good—you know. I'll fail completely and everyone will find me out. If I pull something off, I'm grateful and relieved."

lives of the stars. She's another "one of life's watchers," the female counterpart of Allen in *Play It Again, Sam.* Just as he conversed with an imaginary Bogart in that movie, Farrow here has a romance with Jeff Daniels, a handsome but imaginary screen character who is more real to her than Aiello. "I just met a wonderful new man," she says of Daniels. "Sure he's fictional, but you can't have everything."

When Daniels takes Farrow's hand and draws her into the movie-within-the-movie, she is in seventh heaven. "My whole life I wondered what it would be like to be on this side of the screen," she says. Well, haven't we all? Isn't that exactly what the movies are about?

In the end, though, she chooses real life over fantasy, and puts her faith in Jeff Daniels the actor, instead of in his screen image. "I'm a real person and

Three faces of the ever-versatile Mia Farrow.
Left:
A day-dreaming, plate-dropping waitress in
The Purple Rose of Cairo.
Below:
The unhappy, ever-shopping society matron in *Alice*.
Opposite:
The rags-to-riches cigarette girl in *Radio Days*. Allen wrote and directed but did not appear in any of these films.

Yet she has the courage to risk failure, in much the same way as Allen. He told *Newsweek:* "I think it's important for any filmmaker or playwright to do a lot of stuff and to fail miserably a portion of the time. It's a healthy sign you're trying to grow. So I'm willing to be publicly humiliated."

He took one of his biggest risks in 1978 by making *Interiors,* a serious attempt at drama. He didn't appear in it because he thought that would make audiences think it was a comedy. With Farrow, Allen made the first comedy in which he did not star, *The Purple Rose of Cairo,* because she was able to carry the film without him. And in it she played a classic Allen character: someone overwhelmed by life, preferring fantasy to reality, enraptured by the movies. Married to ne'er-do-well Danny Aiello, she is a failure at love and a flop as a waitress, dropping dishes and mixing up orders. When she gets fired, she heads straight for a matinee. Her life begins and ends in the movie theater; most of her conversations revolve around movie plots and the private

In *Alice* she is more like Allen than ever before. In the *New York Times* Vincent Canby wrote that Mia Farrow plays "what is, in effect, the Woody Allen role, that of someone who is both fearful and determined, both romantic and pragmatic. . . ." Canby also commented: "Alice is a closet-feminist version of the sort of character Mr. Allen usually plays. She is fearful but stubbornly sane, starry-eyed but ever on the lookout for banana peels. In spite of the worldliness around her, she remains hopelessly naive. . . ."

When Farrow and Allen are in the same movie, she is the woman he desires but rarely wins. He loses her to someone else in *A Midsummer Night's Sex Comedy* and *Crimes and Misdemeanors.* They are already divorced at the start of *Hannah and Her Sisters.* They break up in "Oedipus Wrecks," Allen's segment in *New York Stories,* much to the delight of his mother, who considered them mismatched from the start. "How can you marry a blonde with three kids? What are you—an astronaut?" whines Mom. In *Zelig,* Allen and Farrow actually marry and live happily ever after because, for Leonard Zelig: "The love of one woman changed his life." And at the end of *Broadway Danny Rose* they reconcile—certainly they'll be friends, and perhaps someday lovers.

In the films Allen and Farrow have made together, their relationships are more varied and the themes are more profound and much more richly textured than in those he made with Keaton. Perhaps this represents Allen's personal growth as a filmmaker, but in some way, it also seems a reflection of his multifaceted relationship with Farrow.

He has said, for example, that *Broadway Danny Rose* was inspired by Farrow, who told Allen she'd noticed a woman like Tina and wanted to play her on screen. And the happy conclusion of *Hannah and Her Sisters,* in which all three couples have found (or rediscovered) love and, in the process, affirmed traditional family values, may be a reflection of Allen and Farrow's own extended family. (They have two children together, Dylan (by adoption) and Satchel.)

Though Allen still focuses on relationships, his work now reaches deeper levels of understanding about the human condition and the paradoxes of life—mostly cloaked in humor, of course, but given voice nonetheless. "Tell me something," Farrow asks Allen in *A Midsummer Night's Sex Comedy.* "If you lusted after me so, why weren't you in love with me? Can the two feel-

no matter how tempted I am, I have to choose the real world." But Daniels deserts her, and in the final reel she's back in the movie theater, watching Fred Astaire and Ginger Rogers dance across the stage. Conversely, *Play It Again, Sam* ends on a much more upbeat note. Allen realizes a life-long fantasy by reciting the closing lines of *Casablanca* to Keaton. Then he admits to Bogart that "the secret's not being you, it's being me. True, you're not too tall and kind of ugly but, what the hell, I'm short enough and ugly enough myself to succeed on my own." Well, upbeat in a Woody Allen kind of way.

Allen has written and directed four other movies featuring Mia Farrow (not always as the lead character, though) in which he does not appear, *Radio Days* (for which he did the voice-over narration), *Another Woman, September,* and *Alice.* In the two comedies, Farrow is again a female version of Allen. In *Radio Days* she's a cigarette girl struggling to break into broadcasting, for the most part sleeping her way to the top. After a rooftop tryst with a famous radio personality, she delivers a classic Allenesque line: "Boy that was fast! Probably helped that I had the hiccups."

Woody Allen on location in *Radio Days*, a sentimental ode to his Brooklyn childhood. "Forgive me if I tend to romanticize the past," Allen says in voice over. We do.

ings be separate?" Allen raises this question in many of his movies, and here he answers it by noting: "Sometimes I think the two are totally different. Sex alleviates tension and love causes it."

In his pseudodocumentary, *Zelig*, Allen has the chameleon-like ability to transform himself into a replica of anyone around him. Farrow is his psychiatrist. ("She broke with Freud over the concept of penis envy. He thought it was only limited to women.") Through the character of Leonard Zelig, Allen shows how miserable you can make yourself if you try to be like everybody else.

In *Hannah and Her Sisters* Michael Caine addresses the notion that we can never truly understand love. Speaking to a central thesis in Allen's work, he says: "For all my education, accomplishments, and so-called wisdom, I can't fathom my own heart."

Crimes and Misdemeanors, on the other hand, deals with not being able to love the right person. Allen is crazy about Farrow, and they seem perfectly matched. Both intelligent and driven, they work well together, enjoy the same movies, and like the same food. Yet she winds up with Alan Alda, an airhead television

producer. "It's very hard to get your head and heart to work together in life," Allen observes. "In my case, they're not even friendly."

In the same movie Allen deals seriously with the possibility of human happiness. "You've seen too many movies," Martin Landau tells Allen. "I mean, if you want a happy ending, you should go see a Hollywood movie." Yet in *Crimes and Misdemeanors,* Allen is making a documentary about a psychiatrist who takes a more pragmatic view: "Human happiness does not seem to have been included in the design of creation. It is we, with our capacity to love, who give meaning to the indifferent universe. Most human beings seem to have the ability to keep trying and even to find joy from simple things like their family, their work, and from the hope that future generations might understand more." But the psychiatrist is not entirely optimistic, because he later commits suicide, an event that astounds Allen. "When I grew up in Brooklyn, no one committed suicide. They were all too unhappy," he says, masking his horror, as always, with humor.

And in the simply astonishing *Alice,* Farrow embarks on a voyage of inner knowledge. Aided by the potions, herbs, and pipe smoke of Dr. Yang, she acts out her fantasies, becomes invisible, and relives events in her past, confronting ghosts and personal demons. During her odyssey she discovers that her marriage is a sham. The best her husband, William Hurt, can say about her is: "You have a nice personality and you know sweaters." The ghost of her mother appears to tell her: "When it came to me and your dad, you had stars in your eyes." Farrow finally sees that her mother was charming but misguided. She begins an affair with Joe Mantegna, who seems interested in her mainly because "there's nothing sexier than a lapsed Catholic," but then he drops her for his ex-wife. Desperate for solutions, Farrow rushes back to Dr. Yang, but he cannot tell her what to do. "Love is a most complex emotion," says the doctor. "No rational thought . . . much romance, but

Opposite:
A small-time agent with a heart of gold and a head of tin foil, Allen annoys the bleached-blond, gum-chewing Farrow in *Broadway Danny Rose*. She's in love with Allen's client, Lou Canova (Nick Apollo Forte). Against his better judgment, Allen acts as a beard for Forte, pretending to be Farrow's date. Constantly spouting show-biz wisdom, Allen warns crooner Forte: "You can't ride two horses with one behind."

Farrow as Dr. Eudora Fletcher and Allen as Leonard Zelig, with cast members in *Zelig*. She cures
him of his chameleon neurosis. Under hypnosis, he confesses: "I want to go to
bed with you. . . . You're very sweet. Of course, you're not as clever as you think you are. You're all mixed up,
nervous, and you're the worst cook. Those pancakes! Oh, I love you. I want to
take care of you. I don't want pancakes."

much suffering." He has helped her discover her innermost feelings, but his magic cannot provide her with answers. She alone must choose her path.

In all of Allen's work, we are moved by the shock of recognition and the unpredictability of life, which he so deftly captures. His genius for combining the humor and the pathos of the human condition is always fascinating, even in his less successful work. He takes enormous risks, and succeeds or fails in equal proportion. But he always errs on the side of honesty. In an interview for *Time* in 1979 he told Frank Rich: "At the personal level, I try to pay attention to the moral side of issues as they arise and try not to make a wrong choice. For instance, I don't think it's right to try to buy your way out of life's painful side by using drugs. I'm also against the concept of short marriages, and regard my own marriages as a sign of failure of some sort. Of course, I sell out as much as anyone—inside."

At the conclusion of *Manhattan,* Allen is lying on a couch thinking about the "things that make life worth living." Among the items on his list: Groucho Marx, Willie Mays, the second movement of Mozart's "Jupiter" Symphony, *Sentimental Education* by Flaubert, Louis Armstrong's recording of "Potato Head Blues," Swedish films, the crabs at Sam Wu's, Frank Sinatra, Marlon Brando, and those incredible apples and pears by Cézanne. It's an interesting exercise, and it might just surprise this extraordinary filmmaker to learn that many people would include, on their own lists, the films of Woody Allen.

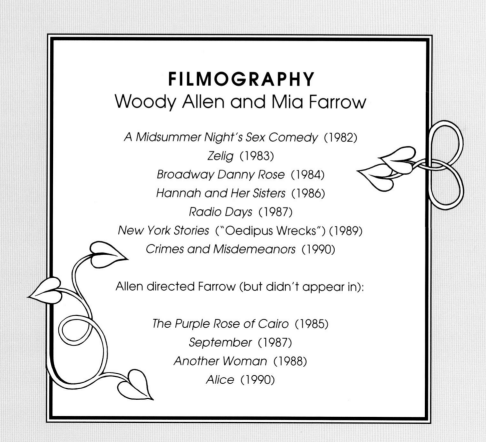

FILMOGRAPHY
Woody Allen and Mia Farrow

A Midsummer Night's Sex Comedy (1982)
Zelig (1983)
Broadway Danny Rose (1984)
Hannah and Her Sisters (1986)
Radio Days (1987)
New York Stories ("Oedipus Wrecks") (1989)
Crimes and Misdemeanors (1990)

Allen directed Farrow (but didn't appear in):

The Purple Rose of Cairo (1985)
September (1987)
Another Woman (1988)
Alice (1990)

197

REFERENCE NOTES

PAGE	REFERENCE
9	"I don't think it's talent, . . ." Clive James, "Clive James Meets Katharine Hepburn" (documentary).
15	"Garbo has only to . . ." David Ansen, *The Divine Garbo* (documentary).
15	"There was something . . ." Frank Martin and Michael Henry Wilson, "Over the Rainbow: The Rise and Fall of MGM" (documentary).
15	"On the screen as off, . . ." Ephraim Katz, *The Film Encyclopedia*, p. 465.
15	"I can't remember being young, . . ." David Ansen, *The Divine Garbo* (documentary).
15	"Tell her in America . . ." Ibid.
17	"I think we've got . . ." Frank Martin and Michael Henry Wilson, "Over the Rainbow: The Rise and Fall of MGM" (documentary).
17	"The most alluring . . ." James Parrish, *Hollywood's Great Love Teams*, p. 49.
18	"She keeps saying . . ." David Ansen, *The Divine Garbo* (documentary).
18	"Your joys and sorrows . . ." Ibid.
18	"But he was the one . . ." Jane Ellen Wayne, *Crawford's Men*, p. 100.
19	"What when drunk . . ." David Ansen, *The Divine Garbo* (documentary).
22	"Possibly the most important factor . . ." Ephraim Katz, *The Film Encyclopedia*, p. 482.
24	"You can't pigeon-hole Garbo . . ." Frank Martin and Michael Henry Wilson, "Over the Rainbow: The Rise and Fall of MGM" (documentary).
24	"Why did you give up . . ." David Niven, *Bring on the Empty Horses*, pp. 460-61.
24	"I never said I want . . ." David Ansen, *The Divine Garbo* (documentary).
24	"Harlow was supposed . . ." Lyn Tornabene, *Long Live the King*, p. 167.
27	"I just got paid . . ." Ralph Bellamy, *When the Smoke Hit the Fan*, pp. 111-12.
29	"When I'd write things like . . ." Lyn Tornabene, *Long Live the King*, p. 168.
31	"Dearest Dear . . ." Irving Shulman, *Harlow: An Intimate Biography*, p. 158.
31	"kid around and wrestle . . ." Lyn Tornabene, *Long Live the King*, p. 168.
35	"Women reproved (Harlow). . ." Irving Shulman, *Harlow: An Intimate Biography*, p. 407.
40	"What woman would deny Clark Gable . . ." Lyn Tornabene, *Long Live the King*, p. 127.
40	"The news of Harlow's death spread . . ." Warren G. Harris, *Gable & Lombard*, p. 77.
40	"I feel like I've been holding a ghost . . ." Ibid., p. 78.
43	"Whatever role she played, . . ." Jane Ellen Wayne, *Crawford's Men*, p. 9.
44	"Joan Crawford is doubtless the best example . . ." Ibid., p. 11.
44	"She was a star . . ." Ibid., p. 131.
44	"it was like an electric current . . ." Warren G. Harris, *Gable & Lombard*, p. 34.
44	"the affair that nearly burned . . ." Ibid.
45	"Because with one of those floozies, . . ." Ibid., p. 64.
45	"We were too much alike . . ." Jane Ellen Wayne, *Crawford's Men*, p. 158.
45	"Few people understood my relation-ship . . ." Ibid.
45	"He's tough, uneducated, . . ." Lyn Tornabene, *Long Live the King*, p. 156.
45	"He pushed women around, . . ." David Shipman, *The Great Movie Stars*, p. 215.
46	"I knew I was falling into a trap . . ." Jane Ellen Wayne, *Crawford's Men*, p. 135.
47	"Kept on insisting that Gable was . . ." David Shipman, *The Great Movie Stars*, p. 215.
47	"a gigolo with . . ." Warren G. Harris, *Gable & Lombard*, p. 36.
48	"He knew where he was the minute he looked . . ." Lyn Tornabene, *Long Live the King*, p. 207.
48	"The first thing he always did . . ." Ibid., p. 208.
48	"He made you feel . . ." Ibid.
48	"The kisses still seem convincing today, . . ." Lyn Tornabene, *Long Live the King*, p. 171.
48	"What makes you think . . ." Warren G. Harris, *Gable & Lombard*, p. 68.
51	"Clark came to me . . ." Jane Ellen Wayne, *Crawford's Men*, p. 189.
51	"Part of me went . . ." Ibid., p. 208.
51	"When a love affair begins, . . ." Ibid., p. 99.
55	"six years of . . ." David Shipman, *The Great Movie Stars*, p. 26.
55	"Rogers was outstanding among . . ." John Mueller, *Astaire Dancing*, p. 8.
55	"She was a great artist, . . ." *Current Biography 1945*, p. 22.
56	"Can't act, can't sing . . ." Arlene Croce, *The Fred Astaire & Ginger Rogers Book*, p. 14.
56	"the best singer of songs . . ." David Shipman, *The Great Movie Stars*, p. 25.
57	"What's all this talk about me . . ." John Mueller, *Astaire Dancing*, p. 8.
59	Achievement unsurpassed. Ibid., p. 10.
60	"He was technically the greatest revolutionary . . ." Arlene Croce, *The Fred Astaire and Ginger Rogers Book*, pp. 135-36.
61	"You would be surprised how . . ." John Mueller, *Astaire Dancing*, p. 15.
61	"I think it's probably the secret . . ." Ibid., p. 18.
61	Golf balls. Paul Boller and Ronald Davis, *Hollywood Anecdotes*, p. 240.
61	Feathered dress. Bob Thomas, *Astaire: The Man, The Dancer*, pp. 129-31.
61	"Just try and keep up with those feet . . ." John Mueller, *Astaire Dancing*, p. 18.
61	"What made the films so popular . . ." David Shipman, *The Great Movie Stars*, p. 26.
62	"Pandro Berman has said . . ." Arlene Croce, *The Fred Astaire & Ginger Rogers Book*, p. 131.
63	"Over the course of his long . . ." John Mueller, *Astaire Dancing*, p. 35.
63	"fifty years from now . . ." David Shipman, *The Great Movie Stars*, p. 25.
68	"Wouldn't you know, . . ." James Kotsilibas-Davis and Myrna Loy, *Being and Becoming*, p. 58.
69	"Venus de Milo at the intersection . . ." Ibid., p. 96.
71	"My first scene with Bill, . . ." Ibid., pp. 87-88.
72	"The whole thing broke with tradition . . ." Ibid., pp. 90-91.
72	"What made The Thin Man series . . ." Ibid., p. 91.
72	"There had been romantic couples . . ." Ibid., p. 70.
72	"the eternal good-sex . . ." Ibid., p. 91.
72	"We became close friends . . ." Ibid.
73	"My friends never fail to . . ." Charles Francisco, *Gentleman: The William Powell Story*, p. 158.
73	"I realized during that trip . . ." James Kotsilibas-Davis and Myrna Loy, *Being and Becoming*, p. 142.
73	"blamed himself for Jean's death . . ." Ibid., p. 150.

PAGE	REFERENCE
77	"announced new Noras . . ." Charles Francisco, *Gentleman: The William Powell Story*, p. 183.
78	"Well, our screen partnership lasted . . ." James Kotsilibas-Davis and Myrna Loy, *Being and Becoming*, p. 322.
78	"Myrna was my heroine, . . ." Ibid., p. 294.
78	"Whenever I'm too crazy, . . ." Cynthia Heimel, "When in Doubt, Act Like Myrna Loy," *But Enough About You*, p. 160.
82	"A singer named Gene Mallin . . ." James Parrish, *The Jeanette MacDonald Story*, p. 79.
83	"I've handled Indians . . ." Ibid., p. 123.
85	"In our films together, . . ." Ibid., p. 131.
86	"The passing of Jeanette MacDonald . . ." Ibid., p. 179.
87	"Indian Love Call" Copyright © 1924 by Harms Inc. (ASCAP).
89	"As a matter of fact . . ." Jack Warner, *My First Hundred Years in Hollywood*, p. 116.
90	"Only lithe, handsome Errol Flynn . . ." Neal Gabler, *An Empire of Their Own*, p. 191.
93	"Adventure on the high seas . . ." Peter Valenti, *Errol Flynn: A Bio-Bibliography*, p. 18.
93	"I was to spend five miserable years . . ." James Parrish, *Hollywood's Great Love Teams*, p. 344.
95	"His ardor for her made acting . . ." Ibid., p. 345.
95	"I had a crush on him . . ." Tony Thomas, Rudy Behlmer, and Clifford McCarthy, *The Complete Films of Errol Flynn*, p. 13.
95	"It was Olivia De Havilland . . ." Penny Stallings, *Flesh and Fantasy*, n. p.
95	"Seeing Robin Hood after all those years . . ." Tony Thomas, Rudy Behlmer, and Clifford McCarthy, *The Complete Films of Errol Flynn*, p. 13.
97	"In 1938 . . . Warners offered . . ." Ibid., p. 86.
97	"Walking through life with you, . . ." David Shipman, *The Great Movie Stars*, p. 200.
97	"I do not depend on Flynn . . ." Tony Thomas, Rudy Behlmer, and Clifford McCarthy, *The Complete Films of Errol Flynn*, p. 40.
98	"An unhappy experience in Hollywood. . . ." Ibid., p. 13.
98	"He was a charming and magnetic man, . . ." Ibid.
101	"Contemporary critics thought he overshadowed . . ." David Shipman, *The Great Movie Stars: The Golden Years*, pp. 230-31.
101	"the little girl with . . ." Ephraim Katz, *The Film Encyclopedia*, p. 467.
102	"When you look at Andy Hardy pictures, . . ." Neal, Gabler, *An Empire of Their Own*, p. 215.
102	"We looked out the window . . ." Ibid., p. 216.
108	"This is the love of my life, . . ." James Parrish, *Hollywood's Great Love Teams*, p. 452.
108	"She just plain . . ." Ephraim Katz, *The Film Encyclopedia*, p. 468.
112	"That handsome piece . . ." David Shipman, *The Great Hollywood Stars*, p. 432.
114	"had the notion that someone . . ." James Parrish, *Hollywood's Great Love Teams*, p. 488.
116	"What makes Mrs. Miniver work . . ." Ibid., p. 489.
118	"I am inclined to think . . ." David Shipman, *The Great Movie Stars*, p. 236.
122	"Favorite pictures? . . ." Ibid., p. 435.
123	"Elders who sigh, . . ." James Parrish, *Hollywood's Great Love Teams*, p. 510.
127	"In my first thirty-four pictures . . ." David Shipman, *The Great Movie Stars*, p. 72.
127	"I'm sick to death . . ." *Current Biography 1942*, p. 91.
128	"cinema personality to burn . . ." Ephraim Katz, *The Film Encyclopedia*, p. 64.
135	"left a fine legacy . . ." David Shipman, *The Great Movie Stars*, p. 75.
139	"I never liked Scarlett, . . ." Ibid., p. 337.
139	"She missed him so dreadfully . . ." Gene Feldman and Suzette Winter, *Vivien Leigh: Scarlett and Beyond* (documentary).
139	"Romance of classic proportions" Ibid.
139	"He was considered an excellent actor . . ." Sewell Stokes, "The Oliviers," p. 711.
140	"I confess I should dearly liked . . ." Garson Kanin, *Together Again!*, p. 188.
140	"It is unfortunate that Vivien's . . ." Ibid.
140	"They really were the King . . ." Gene Feldman and Suzette Winter, *Vivien Leigh: Scarlett and Beyond* (documentary).
140	"racked with worry and guilt; . . ." Virginia Fairweather, *Cry God for Larry*, p. 27.
141	"Poor, dear Vivien" Gene Feldman and Suzette Winter, *Vivien Leigh: Scarlett and Beyond* (documentary).
141	Olivier's work. Scott Siegel and Barbara Siegel, *The Encyclopedia of Hollywood*, p. 310.
141	"The most idyllic of modern . . ." *Current Biography 1946*, pp. 340, 436.
143	"The Burtons at love or war . . ." Keith Botsford, "The White Rolls-Royce," p. 56.
144	"It will be fun to be the first . . ." James Parrish, *Hollywood's Great Love Teams*, p. 770.
144	"Was considered the heir to Olivier . . ." Scott Siegel and Barbara Siegel, *The Encyclopedia of Hollywood*, p. 67.
144	"I found it vulgar, . . ." James Parrish, *Hollywood's Great Love Teams*, p. 772.
146	"Maybe Richard and I are sex symbols . . ." Garson Kanin, *Together Again!*, p. 220.
148	"Her breasts were apocalyptic, . . ." Richard Burton, "Burton Writes of Taylor."
149	"Whether husbands and wives should . . ." Wilfrid Sheed, "Burton and Taylor Must Go."
151	"We cannot just go on . . ." Keith Botsford, "The White Rolls-Royce," p. 58.
153	"I had been making the rounds, . . ." Joe Morella and Edward Z. Epstein, *Paul and Joanne*, p. 19.
156	"When I wasn't playing small, . . ." Ibid., p. 74.
156	"In its sociological aim, . . ." James Parrish, *Hollywood's Great Love Teams*, p. 732.
157	"A winning combination of an athletic physique . . ." Ephraim Katz, *The Film Encyclopedia*, p. 856.
159	"Sort of made up. . . ." Larry Rohter, "Crossing the Bridges with the Newmans."
160	"It's certainly an exciting. . ." Connie Chung, "Face to Face with Connie Chung" (TV interview).
163	"We were the perfect male/female . . ." Clive James, "Clive James Meets Katharine Hepburn" (documentary).
163	"I thought, if I'm a success, . . ." Ibid.
163	"It can frankly be said . . ." David Shipman, *The Great Movie Stars*, p. 275.
163	"the greatest calcium . . ." Paul Boller and Ronald Davis, *Hollywood Anecdotes*, p. 105.

PAGE	REFERENCE
163	"I talk fast and I talk loud . . ." Clive James, "Clive James Meets Katharine Hepburn" (documentary).
163	"I wanted to be William S. Hart, . . ." Ibid.
163	"Hepburn ran the gamut . . ." Ibid.
163	"When I was down in the gutter . . ." Ibid.
163	"The secret of life . . ." Ibid.
164	"I admired him . . ." Ibid.
164	"You're rather *short* . . ." Garson Kanin, *Tracy and Hepburn*, p. 4.
164	"Tracy was one of the few . . ." David Shipman, *The Great Movie Stars*, p. 526.
166	"He never gussied it up. . . ." Ibid., p. 525.
166	"Eddie Robinson, me, Bogie, . . ." Garson Kanin, *Tracy and Hepburn*, p. 239.
166	"The art of acting is . . ." Ibid., p. 7.

PAGE	REFERENCE
166	"He was afraid of going on a bender, . . ." James Kotsilibas-Davis and Myrna Loy, *Myrna Loy: Being and Becoming*, pp. 152-53.
166	"He made the usual play for me . . ." Ibid., p. 154.
166	"I've always liked to live . . ." Garson Kanin, *Tracy and Hepburn*, p. 13.
168	"I don't think I really believed . . ." Charles Higham, *Kate*, p. 113.
173	"The surprising aspect of their joint success . . ." Garson Kanin, *Tracy and Hepburn*, p. 6.
176	"I always felt they gave it . . ." Clive James, "Clive James Meets Katharine Hepburn" (documentary).
176	"IT WAS DELIGHTFUL . . ." Garson Kanin, *Tracy and Hepburn*, p. 28.
176	"I would've loved to . . ." Clive James, "Clive James Meets Katharine Hepburn" (documentary).

PAGE	REFERENCE
177	"He found life difficult. . . ." Ibid.
181	"I feel like I've lucked out . . ." Sam Rubin and Richard Taylor, *Mia Farrow*, p. 109.
181	"When I know a person intimately, . . ." Ibid., p. 108.
182	"A romanticized version" Ibid., p. 117.
187	"I don't have that Jewish . . ." Douglas Brode, *Woody Allen*, p. 36.
187	"It's 85 percent true . . ." Garson Kanin, *Together Again*, p. 244.
187	"eighty percent of the film . . ." Ibid.
188	"I guess what everybody . . ." Douglas Brode, *Woody Allen*, p. 175.
191	"Originally, I asked Mia . . ." Sam Rubin and Richard Taylor, *Mia Farrow*, p. 108.
191	"I was afraid that I would disappoint . . ." Ibid.
191	"I always worry I won't . . ." Ibid., p. 108.

PERMISSIONS

SELECTED BIBLIOGRAPHY

Anger, Kenneth. *Hollywood Babylon II.* New York: Dutton, 1984.

Barker, Felix. *Laurence Olivier.* New York: Hippocrene, 1984.

Bellamy, Ralph. *When the Smoke Hit the Fan.* Garden City, N.Y.: Doubleday, 1979.

Bendazzi, Giannalberto. *The Films of Woody Allen.* Translated by Paul and Christopher Clark. London: Ravette Limited, 1984.

Berg, A. Scott. *Goldwyn.* New York: Knopf, 1989.

Boller, Paul, and Ronald Davis. *Hollywood Anecdotes.* New York: Ballantine, 1987.

Botsford, Keith. "The White Rolls-Royce," *New York Times Magazine,* March 25, 1973, pp. 56-61.

Brode, Douglas. *Woody Allen.* Secaucus, N.J.: Citadel, 1987.

Burton, Richard. "Burton Writes of Taylor," *Vogue,* March 1965, pp. 130-34.

Celebrity Service International. *Earl Blackwell's Entertainment Celebrity Register.* Detroit: Visible Ink, 1991.

Croce, Arlene. *The Fred Astaire and Ginger Rogers Book.* New York: Galahad, 1972.

Current Biography, Cumulative Index 1940-1985. New York: H. W. Wilson, 1986.

Eames, John Douglas. *The MGM Story.* New York: Crown, 1975.

Fairweather, Virginia. *Cry God for Larry: An Intimate Memoir of Sir Laurence Olivier.* London: Calder & Boyars, 1969.

Francisco, Charles. *Gentleman: The William Powell Story.* New York: St. Martin's, 1985.

Friedrich, Otto. *City of Nets.* New York: Harper & Row, 1986.

Gabler, Neal. *An Empire of Their Own: How the Jews Invented Hollywood.* New York: Anchor/Doubleday, 1988.

Hagen, John Milton. *Holly-Would!.* New Rochelle, N.Y.: Arlington House, 1974.

Harris, Warren G. *Gable & Lombard.* New York: Warner Paperback Library, 1975.

Heimel, Cynthia. "When in Doubt, Act Like Myrna Loy," *But Enough About You.* New York: Simon & Schuster, 1986.

Hepburn, Katharine. *The Making of "The African Queen".* New York: Knopf, 1987.

Higham, Charles. *Kate: The Life of Katharine Hepburn.* New York: New American Library, 1975.

Kanin, Garson. *Hollywood.* New York: Viking, 1974.

———. *Together Again!.* New York: Doubleday, 1981.

———. *Tracy and Hepburn.* New York: Primus/Donald I. Fine, 1971.

Katz, Ephraim. *The Film Encyclopedia.* New York: Harper & Row, 1979.

Kotsilibas-Davis, James, and Myrna Loy. *Myrna Loy: Being and Becoming.* New York: Donald I. Fine, 1987.

Lax, Eric. "Woody & Mia," *New York Times,* February 24, 1991, pp. 31-74.

Marx, Samuel. *A Gaudy Spree: Literary Hollywood When the West Was Fun.* New York: Franklin Watts, 1987.

Mordden, Ethan. *Movie Star: A Look at the Women Who Made Hollywood.* New York: St. Martin's, 1983.

Morella, Joe, and Edward Z. Epstein. *Paul and Joanne.* New York: Delacourt, 1988.

Mueller, John. *Astaire Dancing.* New York: Knopf, 1985.

Netter, Susan. *Paul Newman and Joanne Woodward.* New York: Paperjacks, 1989.

Niven, David. *Bring on the Empty Horses.* New York: Dell, 1976.

Parrish, James. *Hollywood's Great Love Teams.* New York: Arlington House, 1974.

———. *The Jeanette MacDonald Story.* New York: Mason/Charter, 1976.

Rohter, Larry. "Crossing the Bridges with the Newmans," *New York Times,* November 18, 1990, pp. 13, 16.

Rubin, Sam, and Richard Taylor. *Mia Farrow.* New York: St. Martin's, 1989.

Sheed, Wilfrid. "Burton and Taylor Must Go," *Esquire,* October 1968.

Shipman, David. *The Great Movie Stars: The Golden Years.* New York: Crown, 1970.

Shulman, Irving. *Harlow: An Intimate Biography.* San Francisco: Mercury House, 1964.

Siegel, Scott, and Barbara Siegel. *The Encyclopedia of Hollywood.* New York: Facts on File, 1990.

Stallings, Penny. *Flesh and Fantasy.* New York: St. Martin's, 1978.

Stokes, Sewell. "The Oliviers," *Theater Arts,* December 1945, pp. 711-18.

Thomas, Bob. *Astaire: The Man, The Dancer.* New York: St. Martin's, 1984.

Thomas, Tony, Rudy Behlmer, and Clifford McCarthy. *The Complete Films of Errol Flynn.* New York: Citadel, 1969.

Tornabene, Lyn. *Long Live the King: A Biography of Clark Gable.* New York: Putnam, 1976.

Van Gelder, Peter. *That's Hollywood.* New York: Harper & Row, 1990.

Valenti, Peter. *Errol Flynn: A Bio-Bibliography.* Westport, Conn.: Greenwood, 1984.

Vickers, Hugo. *Vivien Leigh.* Boston: Little, Brown, 1988.

Warner, Jack L., and Dean Jennings. *My First Hundred Years in Hollywood.* New York: Random House, 1965.

Wayne, Jane Ellen. *Crawford's Men.* New York: St. Martin's, 1988.

Webb, Michael. *Hollywood: Legend and Reality.* Boston: New York Graphic Society/Little, Brown, 1986.

Wilkerson, Tichi, and Marci Bone. *Hollywood Legends: The Golden Years of The Hollywood Reporter.* Los Angeles: Tale Weaver, 1988.

TV DOCUMENTARIES

Ansen, David. *The Divine Garbo,* TNT, produced by Ellen M. Krass, December 3, 1990.

Chung, Connie. "Face to Face with Connie Chung," NBC, November 22, 1990.

Feldman, Gene, and Suzette Winter. *Vivien Leigh: Scarlett and Beyond,* TNT/Turner Pictures, produced by Wombat Productions, October 22, 1990.

James, Clive. *Clive James Meets Katharine Hepburn,* © LWT 1985, LWT: London Weekend Television for Channel Four.

Martin, Frank, and Michael Henry Wilson, "Over the Rainbow: The Rise and Fall of MGM," TNT. Scheduled for 1992.

Schickel, Richard. *Myrna Loy: So Nice To Come Home To,* TNT, produced by Richard Schickel, June 4, 1990.

INDEX